The Rise and Fall of a Middle Power

The Rise and Fall of a Middle Power

Canadian Diplomacy from King to Mulroney

Arthur Andrew

James Lorimer & Company, Publishers
Toronto, 1993

James Lorimer & Company Ltd. acknowledges with thanks the support of the Canada Council, the Ontario Arts Council and the Ontario Publishing Centre in the development of writing and publishing in Canada.

Canadian Cataloguing in Publication Data

Andrew, Arthur, 1915-
   The rise and fall of a middle power : Canadian diplomacy from King to Mulroney

Includes index.
ISBN 1-55028-430-4 (bound) ISBN 1-55028-432-0 (pbk.)

1. Canada - Foreign relations - 1945-   .
I. Title.

FC602.A54 1993   971.064   C93-095334-7
F1034.2.A54 1993

James Lorimer & Company Ltd., Publishers
Egerton Ryerson Memorial Building
35 Britain Street
Toronto, Ontario M5A 1R7

Printed and bound in Canada

Contents

For J
Love 24+
A

Acknowledgements

For a small book there are many people to thank, beginning with the students who came to my classes at the King's College School of Journalism between September of 1978 when it all started and April of 1993 when we had our last meeting. It was they who forced me to keep in touch with the incredible things that were going on in what is sometimes called the real world. Then there are Marion Fry, President of King's, and Michael Cobden, Director of the School of Journalism, who provided time and space for whatever I wanted to do, as did their predecessors, John Godfrey and Walter Stewart, who added some much needed encouragement. Thank you one and all.

Most of all, I should acknowledge colleagues and friends, often the same people, of the Department of External Affairs between 1947 and 1979, especially Ed Ritchie. He, as Undersecretary, took a chance in bringing me up into the rarified atmosphere of the eighth floor of the Pearson Building and thereby provided a view of the world this book is about.

Some of the arguments presented here about the possible roles of the UN in the Persian Gulf and in the former Yugoslavia first appeared in *Policy Options* and in *The Canadian Forum*.

Then there is the publisher, Jim Lorimer, who saw the book in a wider context than its author did, the editor, Diane Young, who gave it shape, and the freelance editor, Cy Strom, who made it fit to print.

And finally those nearest and most long-suffering — my family, both nuclear and extended, especially my wife, Joyce, and Hilary Sircom, both of whom made the end product more readable than it would otherwise have been. Their relief at seeing it published will be almost as great as my own.

A. J. A.

Introduction

When I retired from the Department of External Affairs at the end of 1979 I had no intention of writing any memoirs. It was a time for something new. In gratitude for my quitting a year before I actually had to, the Department sent me to be Foreign Service Visitor at the University of King's College in Halifax, where the President, John Godfrey, was looking for people to staff the newly established School of Journalism. There would be quite enough to do; if I found time for more I'd write novels!

The change in heart began with trying to teach. First there was a course on what was called "Diplomatic Reporting," not what diplomats reported home but what journalists wrote about international affairs. Later there was "Background to the News," which I used to say was a course on "Elementary Cynicism" until I found it was being taken seriously.

Trying to give students practice in looking behind the press releases and the headlines obliged me to keep up with the events that reshaped our world during the eighties and particularly those affecting Canada's place in it. Teaching made me curious about what was going on in my former line of work and pushed me to be more analytical than I would otherwise have been. Well before the fateful 1988 election it had become clear that the most fundamental assumptions on which Canada's foreign policy had been based since even before we knew we had a foreign policy were no longer regarded as valid. And the worst part was that this had happened without those assumptions ever being publicly challenged, much less debated. The importance of a balance in our relations with the United States, the significance of the United Nations, the value of the Commonwealth and the British connection as a counterpoise and the need for Canada to be seen by other countries as different from the United States, all these "givens" were demoted to the status of secondary interests. Not disavowed but marginalized.

Moreover, all these changes seemed to be in one direction, toward what used to be called "continentalization"; toward policies, mostly business-driven, of greater dependence on the United States, and not just in terms of trade and investment but for wisdom and foresight on the great international issues of the day. It was as if the government was courting fulfilment of Canada's "manifest destiny" to become, if not yet a part of the United States, then certainly a client to it.

Canada, the prototype if not the inventor of the Middle Power concept, was changing its self-perception. Instead of a tough-minded and reasonably independent international operator, we were becoming the ideal team player, one that identified itself more as a member of an alliance than as an actor in its own right on the world scene, sometimes in minor roles, occasionally the star. Where once we had struggled to maintain a balance in our policies between those of an active Middle Power and those of a loyal ally, we no longer seemed interested.

The more the fundamental nature of these changes became apparent, the more obvious it became that they had not suddenly happened in the few years since my retirement. The process must have started while I was still active in the Department. What was more shocking, I probably had taken part in bringing some of them about.

It goes against the grain for one who had thriven under the rule of public service anonymity to come out and declare himself. However, since this book draws heavily on personal experiences, the reader has a right to know whose opinions these are, how reliable the information is and what the judgements are based on.

My involvement with the Department of External Affairs began when I arrived home from the wars in September of 1945 to meet the responsibilities of a wife and child (with a second to be added). When I joined the army in 1939 I was working for the Canadian Press and could have gone back to it. Joyce, my wife, had other ideas, one of which took the form of an application to join something called "External Affairs." All I really knew about it was that a brother of a friend of my brother worked for it. I wrote the exam that fall and although I miraculously passed the written exam, I was told that my BA degree from Dalhousie was so unimpressive they wouldn't have me.

Living with and off my in-laws, I used my veteran's allowance to go back to Dalhousie for an MA. There I was lucky enough to be tutored, in effect, by Professor R.A. MacKay who had served in the Department during the war and who went back to it that same year. The next time I wrote the exam, I was accepted.

I reported to the East Block in Ottawa on August 1, 1947, and, probably because my security check had not been completed, was sent to Protocol Division administering the privileges and immunities of the Ottawa diplomatic corps. After a few months, presumably cleared, I went to European Division to be the original occupant of the German desk and look after Canada's relations with Germany which, as I grandly told my friends, had previously been the job of the Canadian armed forces.

In 1950, I was posted to the Canadian Military Mission in Berlin, but before we arrived there the decision had been made to open a Canadian Diplomatic Mission in Bonn. That was where we settled among the ruins.

I had three memorable jobs in Germany. The first was to plan for the evacuation of Canadians from Germany in the event the Korean War spread to Europe. The second was to collect information concerning "occupation costs" so that the Canadian forces, soon to return to Germany, could "pay their own way" rather than live off the defeated Germans as all our Nato allies were doing. The third was as an observer at the early meetings at Strasbourg of the Council of Europe, where one took cocktails with the likes of Paul-Henri Spaak, Winston Churchill, Harold Macmillan and Mr Europe himself, Guy Mollet.

In January of 1953, to our great delight I was sent to Vienna to open a legation as chargé d'affaires — i.e., my own boss. It was the Vienna of *The Third Man* and the Four-Men-In-A-Jeep could be seen parked on the Kaertnerstrasse. The city was surrounded by Soviet soldiers, the Korean War was still threatening to spread and the Viennese were very glad to see friendly foreigners. It was a broadening personal experience and in terms of professional interest it was my first direct encounter with the mythical Reds and an opportunity to observe the pathos of Displaced Persons and our own immigration process in action.

In 1954 we returned to Ottawa where I headed a new Political Coordination Section with responsibility for advising the CBC International Service on the actual (or probable) policy of the Canadian government on anything the CBCIS might be beaming across the Iron Curtain. Thereafter I became Head of Information Division with responsibility for the projection of Canada abroad including, at that time, cultural matters. In that capacity I had a hand in preparing the Order in Council setting up the Canada Council to ensure that the international interests of Canada's artistic communities would be handled by people whose interests would be less ephemeral.

In 1957, one year after the suppression of the Hungarian uprising and a time when relations with the countries of the Soviet Empire were at their chilliest, we were sent to Prague. It was considered such a hardship post that the legation (there was no question of an embassy) was headed by a chargé d'affaires who was rewarded with all the perks of a proper head of mission: residence, car and driver (that ultimate symbol of status). The three years in Prague (with responsibility for liaison with Budapest) were not easy. Fourteen microphones were taken out of the chancery just as we arrived and we lived with servants who were required to report our every activity to the secret police. We were followed when we left town, and sometimes while we were in it, in what was really an attempt to make our lives as miserable as possible. As can happen, the result was often just the opposite and the diplomatic corps in Prague did have its moments of high, perhaps hysterical, gaiety.

I left Czechoslovakia with one clear impression — that in this the most loyal Soviet satellite, even those attempting to run the so-called communist system did not believe in it and were not at all interested in making it work at more than a subsistence level.

Returning to Ottawa in 1960, I had been promised what was for me the best imaginable job, Head of European Division. Unhappily, the person I was to succeed declined to accept his posting and eventually chose to leave the Department. I was pressed into service for a quick hatchet job, looking after relations with France during the Algerian debate in the UN, in which we may well have offended General de Gaulle enough to account for his later intrusion into Canadian domestic affairs. France gave up Algeria rather than face an adverse vote in the UN and I was made Inspector-General, bribed by an offer of an embassy after a year on that job.

Inspecting was fascinating work but so physically exhausting I eventually came down with boils. Flying on weekends and working weekdays we did inspections of posts in Europe (including, oddly, Prague, which I had just left), the Far East including Indochina, and consular missions in the United States. I also did an internal inspection of the departmental records system and looked into the eventual use of computers.

As a reward for being a good soldier, in 1962 I was appointed Ambassador to Israel and concurrently High Commissioner to Cyprus. Things were quiet in Israel at the time but Cyprus was soon aflame and I spent most of my last year and a half in that area in Nicosia. As the first Canadian UN contingent arrived I was instructed to open a full-time office in Nicosia, and for the first and last time in my experience I was given carte blanche to get what was needed by way of accommodation, vehicles and office supplies, and to pay for it without further reference to Ottawa.

Although there had been some Canadian peacekeepers in Israel, this was my first contact with any significant number of the military since I had myself been one of them. It renewed my high regard for Canadian soldiers, their humanity, their humour, their professionalism and their non-pompous sincerity about what they were doing.

From Israel and Cyprus, I was cross-posted to Sweden, the first time to go from one post to another without a stay in Ottawa. Stockholm turned out to be the scene of perhaps the most interesting and demanding operation of my career — the opening of negotiations with the People's Republic of China. It was a textbook operation involving many members of the Department as well as representatives of other departments, and it did much to enhance Canada's reputation as an independent operator while serving the interests of the international community and, at least potentially, Canada's own commercial interests as well.

While on post in Stockholm I headed Canada's delegation in Geneva to the United Nations Conference on Trade and Development (UNCTAD). In a display of virtuosity unsupported by any technical qualifications on the subject, I led our delegation to the 1967 Stockholm conference on copyrights and patents. Margaret Meagher succeeded me in the summer of 1969.

About this time Marcel Cadieux, the Undersecretary, was swapping jobs with Ed Ritchie, our man in Washington. During the transition in Ottawa, which coincided with a pause in the Chinese negotiations in Stockholm, I was sent to the University of Toronto to be, as someone said, Ambassador to Jim Eayres, the U of T professor who was then a frequent and acerbic commentator on the Department's activities. While at Toronto and with the encouragement of John Holmes, then president of the Canadian Institute for International Affairs, I wrote a thin book called *Defence by Other Means; Diplomacy for the Underdog,* which the CIIA published.

Our stay in Toronto was shortened by some months and I was called back to Ottawa in the early spring of 1970 to be Head of Far Eastern Division and soon after Director-General of the newly created Asia and Pacific Bureau. In these capacities and under the wise and jaded eye of Ralph Collins, Assistant Undersecretary, I managed the Ottawa end of the Chinese negotiations, the ultimate establishment of relations with Peking and the difficult withdrawal of recognition from the regime on Taiwan.

Early in 1971, as part of a tour of my new area of responsibility, I went to Peking to see our new embassy then being set up by John Fraser. Later that year I became a member of the Canadian Delegation to the United Nations for the debate on the admission of Peking to the UN's China seat. There I saw the process concluded that had started in Stockholm three years earlier.

In 1973 I was loaned to a firm of consultants, Woods, Gordon of Toronto, who had been retained to advise the Department on the location and construction of a new Canadian embassy in Washington. Having fantasized over — or actually acquired — chanceries, residences, or both, in every capital in which I'd been posted, the challenge of the Washington embassy was too much. I immediately went there on my own and wandered around until I saw a property occupied by a dilapidated department store touching on Pennsylvania Avenue.

The statement the new embassy should make, in my view, was that the people represented by it "see themselves as probably the most important country in the world so far as Washington is concerned." The location, on the main parade avenue of the American capital, certainly was consistent with that view. Eventually the consultants agreed to the site, although many years were to pass before it was acquired and a building erected on it.

As Director-General of Asia and the Pacific I was heavily involved in the process that led to the final withdrawal of Canada from the futile international commissions for control and supervision in Vietnam. I accompanied Mitchell Sharp when he visited the area prior to announcing that we would not be continuing our participation in the ICCS. After some twenty years of frustration Canadian military and foreign service people were at last able to leave the scene and to do so before the ultimate fiasco occurred.

I was part of the entourage of Mr Trudeau when he went to China in October of 1973, to Washington to discuss energy with Gerald Ford in 1974, and to the Caribbean in 1975 just before the Commonwealth Heads of Government meeting in Jamaica. On two occasions I travelled abroad from Ottawa for special jobs: once as a member of the Canadian delegation to a senior officials' meeting of the Commonwealth in London and once to Moscow to lead the Canadian team negotiating terms for the implementation of Mr Trudeau's protocol for cultural exchanges with the USSR.

Early in 1974, I was appointed Assistant Undersecretary of State for External Affairs (AUSSEA) and was given an area of interest that included most of the geographical bureaus in the Department as well as the divisions responsible for the UN and the Commonwealth. John Halstead was the senior AUSSEA and retained responsibility for Europe and Nato. John was fully occupied negotiating the Contractual Link with Europe, whose purpose was to have the EEC treat Canada and the USA as distinct economic entities instead of lumping them together for purposes of statistics and tariffs as the EEC had recently begun to do.

This was the situation when Ed Ritchie took ill and Basil Robinson was appointed Undersecretary. A little while after Basil was installed, I told him that having had seven good but strenuous years in Ottawa and considering that he might like to have his own nominee in my place, I was ready for a posting abroad. Basil eventually made a number of attractive suggestions, the most attractive of which was Athens.

During my stay in Ottawa (1969–1976) I had been heavily involved in the process of trying to give effect to the new concepts of governmental management espoused by Mr Trudeau. Perhaps with more enthusiasm and loyalty than wisdom, I entered very much into the spirit of change that was characteristic of the time. Although, like many of my colleagues, I considered some of the proposals for management by objectives to be patent nonsense, I agreed with most of what was being done. Many of the changes were overdue and necessary in spite of the ideology that came with them.

Nevertheless, in retrospect, I was naïve in seeing the process as a mere administrative rationalization of the government's foreign operations to make them more responsive to the needs of the other departments that operated outside Canada, especially Industry, Trade and Commerce. The moves that led up to the creation of the super-department now known as External Affairs and Foreign Trade Canada did not ring the alarm bells they should have. I am not at all sure that the result we have today was the one that Mr Trudeau and his managerial advisors had in mind.

Ed Ritchie, as Undersecretary, was the only person in authority to my knowledge who foresaw what could (and did) happen. The rest of us assumed that any new super-department would be led by its External Affairs element, that the views of the people who oversee the country's broad political interests would always take precedence over those responsible for our sectoral interests, no matter how important. As is now obvious, we were wrong in this assumption.

After two and a half interesting years in Greece, we were told we would have to give up the comfortable residence on the outskirts of Athens for what might be described as technical reasons. Since Joyce and I had spent enough of our life together in house hunting and moving, the prospect of doing it all once more was too daunting. One evening, returning from a particularly deadly diplomatic cocktail party, we collapsed in our chairs and said "enough."

We returned to Canada in the early summer of 1978 and moved to Nova Scotia where we had had a summer place by the sea for many years. In September I went to work at King's, first as Foreign Service Visitor, then as Visiting Professor and finally as Honorary Professor.

The point of this extended curriculum vitae is to present my credentials in making the observations that follow. I was never a member of any inner circle, I made no great decisions of my own, but I was in the neighbourhood of both. I knew, worked and travelled with members of the political and bureaucratic inner circles. For good or ill, I contributed to some of the fateful decisions and helped to implement others.

It was only after leaving the Foreign Service (yet keeping up with later developments) that I began to see the broader picture; to understand, as students say, where the country was coming from, internationally speaking, and to see where it was going. That is the story I try to tell here in the hope that this account of life in External Affairs, of how the Department functioned over a crucial thirty-year period, will show how we reached the present state and suggest what can be done about it.

The working title of this book was "The Dear Department," an "in" joke but not very descriptive. As a sort of relic, wherever External Affairs is being referred to, the use of "the Department" (capitalized) has been retained.

Arthur Andrew,
University of King's College,
Halifax, N.S.
September 1993

Avant-Propos

Not everyone was overjoyed when, in 1973, the Department of External Affairs finally took up residence in the brand new Lester B. Pearson Building on Sussex Drive. After years of inconvenience the Department was at long last leaving those dozen or more holes-in-the-wall scattered all over Ottawa. From now on its members would be dealing face to face with people they had known only by name and telephone number. But it was also leaving the Hill and the offices in the East Block where Sir Joseph Pope, the first Undersecretary, had brought the Department into existence. There were reservations, if not forebodings.

Paul Martin, as Secretary of State for External Affairs, had resisted all attempts to move his department away from the centre of things. Right up to the last moment, his successor, Mitchell Sharp, had managed to hang on to offices in the East Block for himself and his Undersecretary, then Ed Ritchie. Even on departure, Ed had been able to bring one of the sacred relics with him to his new office, high in the Pearsoneum: the enormous undersecretarial desk at which all his predecessors had worked, from Pope and Skelton to Robertson, Pearson, Wilgress, Heeney, Léger and Cadieux. It was said to have been the desk on which Sir John A. Macdonald had been laid after he had passed out for what was to be the last time.

Those in the Department who had been separated from their leaders by the busiest traffic artery in Ottawa were looking forward to the prospect of being able to attend departmental meetings after nothing more eventful than an elevator ride. Others were not so sure. Hadn't Professor Parkinson, bureaucracy's own philosopher, pointed out that the very year the India Office got its own home in Whitehall, the Indian Empire went out of business? Wasn't Paul Martin right? Would External carry as much weight, a mile away and out of sight of the Prime Minister's Office and Parliament, as it had when its bright young people could be watched running for their lives on Wellington Street?

Leaving the Hill for the periphery was at least symbolic of External's change in status. By 1973, the Once-and-Future-Department was no longer what it had been twenty-five years before. When it moved from the centre of Ottawa, External had not been near the centre in government thinking for some time. The move had really begun at least a decade before when John Diefenbaker swept into office, bringing with him, among his many biases, the conviction that the Foreign Service was a Liberal conspiracy—"the Pearsonalities," as he called them. And when Pearson himself succeeded Dief, the Department recovered only some of its former status. Golden Ages are ephemeral things even when they're not followed by goats grazing amid the ruins. By the mid-sixties External was well into middle age—still very good at what it did but inclined to obesity and no longer sure what its goals really were.

The arrival of Pierre Trudeau in the Prime Minister's Office was a much greater shock to the Department's system than the arrival of John Diefenbaker had been. Trudeau had clearly taken the Department's measure and found it wanting. He had also brought with him a fascination with the mechanics, as distinct from the content, of government. He did shake up the Department and did rationalize some of its activities. At the same time he by-passed it, putting some of its functions into other hands and mining its personnel rosters for talent to use in other areas. It was not, however, a total emasculation. External continued to be responsible for running the many aspects of foreign affairs that did not particularly interest the Prime Minister. Moreover, from force of habit if nothing else, it continued for some time to be the place where the government's activities abroad were brought together, inspected and packaged before delivery.

In the Department's heyday, the late forties and early fifties, Ottawa was not much of a city. God and Colonel By had done their part (three rivers, two waterfalls and a canal) but the inhabitants had done little with their inheritance. There were the Parliament Buildings, including the beloved East Block, romantic but out of fashion and not very highly regarded. (One of the original structures on the Hill, the old Supreme Court building, would be torn down to provide parking space.) Off the Hill, the most important buildings were "war temporaries." One housed National Defence, another the wartime controlling agencies. A third, Laurentian Terrace, was maybe the world's largest women's dormitory, home to the hundreds of young women who had come to Ottawa to help win the war and had stayed on.

The intervening years have been kind to Ottawa as, indeed, has the Canadian taxpayer. It is now possibly the best capital in the world in which to be a foreign diplomat. By the same token, it has become more difficult for the Department to persuade its young-married-with-two-children foreign service people to give up life at home for the undoubted delights of Ouagadougou. The interesting thing is that some very bright people still compete for the privilege of making that choice. Hundreds of the brightest and best university graduates in Canada "try for External" every year knowing that their chances are less than one in a hundred of making the cut to qualify for the next stage.

This is no place to examine the psyche of the average Canadian, whoever she might be, but there is a strong streak of the missionary running through most of the breed. They like to travel and are very good at it; good enough that some otherwise patriotic Americans stitch Canadian flags to their rucksacks when they travel outside North America.

Besides making a career of the things Canadians like to do most — preach, teach and travel — there is another factor that contributes to the flow of recruits, the cachet that still seems to go with membership in the Department of External Affairs. Consequently, in spite of its many vicissitudes, the Dear Department continues to appeal to the imaginations of the young people of the country.

Much has been written about various aspects of the Department's work. It has been well described structurally and functionally. Organization charts and personnel statistics, however, fail to convey the feel of the place or the attitudes of the people inside it during what now seem to have been its best years. How did the machine work? How did its people perceive it? How did it fare as an instrument of policy under various governments?

This book tries to report what it was like inside the Department of External Affairs during the golden years when its reputation was high and Canada was cutting quite a figure as a Middle Power on the international scene. It goes on to record the Department's reaction to changes that included the Diefenbaker earthquake, its glide into middle age, and its encounter with Pierre Trudeau, who changed the Department's character. By the time Mr Trudeau left, what had been an influential central government agency led by politically minded idealists had been converted into an operating department of government dominated by economic determinists. This change in the Department's character was followed swiftly by a change in government, from a detached, philosophically inclined Pierre Trudeau, through the interregnum of Joe Clark, to the hands-on wheeler-dealership of Brian Mulroney. The story concludes with an assessment of the role to be played by a secretariat of professional diplomatists serving the government of a country such as Canada with its unique external interests. Judgements are made on how the Department played, failed to play, and might again play a central role in the preservation and advancement of this unique country and of the things it has come to stand for in the world. While looking at the past we should be thinking about the future.

This is a piece of reporting and advocacy, not scholarship. Every effort has been made to verify impressions but many of them remain just the impressions of someone who was in the neighbourhood of the actions described, knew most of the people involved and tried to keep in touch with what was going on.

Only in Canada would it be necessary to justify the way in which a foreign country is discussed. What will seem to some as a thread of anti-Americanism running through the book is, in truth, no such thing. The United States has had a large part in the story. Its motives have been looked at and its actions assessed with objectivity, as if it were any other country. Some of the judgements made will not appear flattering while others might seem bent over backwards. All are intended to present the point of view of a next-door neighbour who is very glad to live in the neighbourhood but who has his own interests and his own outlook to consider.

With the exception of a few very wise individuals, people working in the Department of External Affairs during the late sixties and early seventies failed to observe that responsibility for the conduct of the country's foreign operations was being taken out of the hands of its professional diplomatists. It went first to centralizing methodologists, soon to be succeeded by economically driven ideologues. Both failed to realize that no matter who conducts a country's foreign relationships, the basic facts on which foreign policies must stand cannot be legislated to fit preconceived ideas. John Diefenbaker could not redirect trade by political fiat in 1957 and his successors cannot change the social and cultural basis of the country to suit their commercial agendas. Eventually all the relevant factors involved in an international relationship will be brought to bear in one way or another. The things that make Canada the country it is will either be changed or they will force changes in policy. Policies are easier to change than national characteristics.

There is probably no way to describe the Department, the way it worked and the people in it without laying it open to charges of élitism. It might be better to confess to the charge and plead extenuating circumstances. It was a time when all countries were represented by the same class of people, give or take a few that had not yet produced an educated upper middle class. The two went together. No doubt the "clubbiness" that will be noted could not have existed had it been otherwise. Within these limitations the Foreign Service was broadly representative of the country except in two areas. The first was in the small number of women who were part of it and the second was in the underrepresentation of French-speaking Canada. The small number of women was part of a larger phenomenon. For the underrepresentation of francophones there is less excuse.

The choice of the topics to be covered in some detail may seem puzzling. It is simply a reflection of the writer's personal involvement in the activity of the Department. Similarly, examples used to illustrate general propositions have been drawn mostly from personal experience.

The Age of Innocence
1945–1956

1

The Dear Department

By the time World War II ended in the spring of 1945 Ottawa had attracted to it a very high proportion of the brightest, most energetic, best educated and most highly motivated people that Canada could produce. The armed forces had been asked to give up selected individuals to help prepare for the peace that had been in sight since the successful landing in Europe the previous summer. More than its fair share of this talent went to the Department of External Affairs. "The Department," as it was known to its own, or "External," as it was known around Ottawa, was at the heart of the public service.

During the wartime years External Affairs acted as the government's line of communication with its allies. With its growing number of diplomatic missions abroad, External was the instrument through which the government learned what its allies were thinking of the peace to come. It stimulated and absorbed the government's own thinking, prepared its responses and then conducted the negotiations to narrow any gaps that separated Canada from its allies. When the war ended, External continued to play a similar and central role in all aspects of government policy that had any foreign content.

The Department was also very close to the centre of the government, physically. It occupied part of the same building that housed the Prime Minister, the Cabinet Secretariat, the Privy Council Office and ("Where your treasure is, there will your heart be also") the Department of Finance. The East Block, one of the original Gothic Revival Parliament buildings, was a very cosy place, particularly before it underwent any of its many renovations. The marble fireplaces worked and so did the sinks concealed behind the red velvet curtains that hung from curved brass rods. The building itself exuded solidity and even with four desks in the offices intended for no more than two, it provided a perfect atmosphere for would-be diplomats. People who worked together in that atmosphere came to know each other very well and very often colleagues also became close friends.

External was not universally loved in Ottawa, but because of the esteem in which it and many of its members were held by the government, it had to be respected. The Department, however, was greatly loved by its own. Despite its modest efforts to hide the fact, its self-love no doubt contributed to its subsequent difficulties.

Although the Department may have been the largest single accumulation of intellect in Ottawa, it had nothing like a monopoly. Finance and the Privy Council Office could always claim their fair share of leading lights. C.D. Howe, the Lord-High-Everything-Else of the wartime cabinet, had gathered around him, particularly in the Department of Trade and Commerce, a high-powered band of go-getters, some with academic distinctions but also many who had made their way in business. The External crowd fitted in well with the academics but less so with the business types, many of whom were in Ottawa strictly for "the duration"; as the war wound down, so did their numbers. Those who stayed on regarded the Externalites as interesting, even necessary, but oversold, with influence out of all proportion to their importance in the "real world." Thus began the tension that existed between External and the Department of Trade and Commerce until the two merged in the early eighties.

Within a year or two after the war the higher public service in Ottawa was a coterie of well-qualified, relatively young, mostly male and anglophone intellectuals who soon became known as the mandarins. They had the confidence of Mackenzie King's government, with whom most of them had worked long and hard during the war years. They had confidence in themselves and for the most part they were personal friends as well as professional colleagues. They were also attuned to the priorities of the government of the day and must have appeared to those outside the Liberal Party as virtually inseparable from it. But they did not see themselves as partisan in any sense. They did the government's bidding, which happened to coincide closely with their own inclinations, thanks to the circumstances of the times and to their own considerable influence on government decisions. Mandarin and politician would have agreed that Canada's situation was such that there really was only one sensible policy and it was irrelevant whether any particular piece of policy originated at the political or at the public service level. Moreover, the collegial approach within the public service was so highly developed that by the time a policy was turned into legislation, it was indeed a wise father who knew his own intellectual child.

Those members of the Department who were not full members of the mandarinate saw themselves as cadets destined to join it. If asked what they were doing in Ottawa they would reply, "I work for External," spoken flatly without any inflection that might suggest they expected the questioner to be impressed, which of course they did. If they were then asked what they did in External, the reply was properly, "I'm an FSO." The initials stood for Foreign Service Officer. To call oneself a diplomat was the worst of solecisms; first, because in Ottawa diplomats were by definition foreigners, and second, because calling oneself a diplomat would have been like calling oneself a hero, in the army. Perhaps "diplomatist" but never "diplomat." Many years later when the Department sent members to universities for an academic visitation there was a great debate. The universities wanted to call them "diplomats in residence." External insisted that they should be "foreign service visitors," except in no-nonsense French where precision took priority over false modesty.

When one joined External, families joined too. In the late forties, and for many years afterwards, wives were, in effect, hired along with their husbands. They weren't paid, of course, but they were very obviously considered by the Department to be part of the contract. As the wife of the Undersecretary in 1947, Maryon Pearson used to give teas for the new wives, to which the wives of one or two cabinet ministers would come to welcome and look over the new bunch.

There was, of course, no question of male spouses, although there were a handful of female Foreign Service Officers. It was assumed that these women would either remain celibate or resign. Wives of diplomats of most countries were in an ambivalent position. Legally they were not public servants and never took any of the oaths of office and secrecy. However, wives not only overheard things that would never be said in the presence of any other "unindoctrinated" person, but they were also often used by the diplomat-spouse as a sounding board and confidante in ways that violated all the rules of security, not to mention oaths of office. There were occasions on posts abroad when wives helped their diplomatic spouses decipher telegrams, a job supposedly reserved for those with the highest security clearance.

Some wives enjoyed their unofficial role, but for others classified information was a burden they'd rather not have had to carry. The "need-to-know" rule that governs the dissemination of classified information applied to wives and, sworn or not, they came to know quite a few dark secrets, especially on Iron Curtain posts. It could hardly have been otherwise. They were often at the centre of things, creating an environment conducive to the exchange of information and listening to the process while it was going on. On some posts, wives were much more familiar with what the local secret police, which included domestic servants, were up to than their diplomat husbands. They usually heard more local gossip and, through the household help, felt the direct effects of police curiosity about what went on in embassy households, especially the bedrooms.

Security people are bound to take an interest in the backgrounds of those married to people in positions of trust. For many years, anyone in the Department who wanted to get married required the Undersecretary's approval of the fiancée on security grounds. Although the ability of a wife to keep up the social side of diplomatic life would also have been looked at, this could not have been a decisive factor. Wives came from most social strata in Canada and, like their husbands, learned their trade the hard way, by practising it.

The total effect was to make External a social as well as a public service institution; inward-looking and self-conscious but, with a few exceptions, aware of the dangers of overt élitism in an egalitarian society like Canada. The people who were the role-models of the Department were down-to-earth and hard-working public servants. The Department did try to broaden the outlook of its people by sending FSOs on temporary assignments to other departments while people from other government agencies came to work in the Department. Nevertheless, there was a good deal of self-satisfaction in the Department and it was was only partially offset by an awareness of the risks that came with it.

For many years the Department's Achilles' heel was administration, which was in practice almost entirely divorced from the Department's main activity. The link between those who controlled the purse strings and those who made policy decisions was tenuous at best. Those who looked after money matters and personnel management, the top managers who would have been appalled by the description, were usually FSOs who had agreed to move out of the mainstream to do their share of the dirty work. This situation persisted, for good or ill, until the Trudeau managerial revolution got under way in 1969.

The fact that the show stayed on the road administratively was largely due to a few good women, once buried in the clerical jobs, who rose to take charge. The most famous of these was the keeper of the Department's purse strings, Agnes McCloskie. She was much maligned, but she ran a tight fiscal ship. Expense accounts were really accountable and allowances were so grudgingly allowed that the Dominion Bureau of Statistics had to be enlisted to persuade the Department's own financial controllers that the demands for money to survive in remote corners of the world were not entirely the product of fertile and self-serving imaginations.

At the working level, most of the people who provided the Department with the goods and services it needed to keep it running were members of this dedicated, intelligent and long-suffering group of women — a part of Ottawa's wartime inheritance. Although they were not treated equitably, they were deeply appreciated even when being taken for granted. There were only a handful of women doing FSO work in the early fifties: among them, Dorothy Burwash in economics; Elizabeth MacCallum, an Arabist; Margaret Meagher, a generalist of the mainstream; Laura Beattie and Mary Dench, pillars of the Information Division. But working alongside these few were a host of women who saw that the backwaters of the Department kept the mainstream in business.

One of the continuing debates within the Department concerned the relative merits of the "specialist" or "expert" as compared to the "generalist" and why External preferred the generalist. The whole argument was, in retrospect, entirely semantic. The Department's position was not so much that generalists were more useful than specialists but that the generalism of diplomacy was itself a specialty. Diplomats (when they'd dared to use the term) were a class of experts whose talents had to include briefability — a talent for absorbing the expertise of others and applying it in negotiation on the international scene. Apart from briefability and a knowledge of the foreign environment, the Department never claimed to have its own expertise in all the areas in which it worked. Other government departments active in the international field could not give up their own responsibilities just because the business at hand involved a foreign country. Consequently, management of Canada's external interests was always a matter of careful co-operation in which External was able to maintain ultimate responsibility while being largely governed by the specialist department concerned.

The ideal External FSO had to start with a flexible mind that was able to absorb the essentials of an issue. He was then expected to pick up by exposure the often elaborate rules by which the international community ran its affairs and, eventually, to be able to put it all together and conduct a negotiation. Most FSOs had some specialist qualifications in their background (economics, science, languages, law) but these were secondary to the ability to deal with subjects other than their own. Underlying all of this, the Canadian diplomat's stock-in-trade had to include a solid background knowledge of basic Canadian attitudes and interests. It was only through an understanding of the country that he could extrapolate on his instructions which, in the days of hand cipher, could leave quite a bit to the imagination of the person receiving them.

"Diplomacy" has the same origin in Greek as "duplicity" has in Latin and diplomats are by the nature of their work two-faced, one face looking inward toward home, the other outward toward the world that is their workplace. Diplomats abroad are licensed foreign agents and quite properly seen as such by the people they are sent to live among. At the same time, they often appear back home to be advocates of foreign interests. This in itself is not likely to make anyone popular; but if the unpopularity of diplomats needs further explanation, they are the last legally privileged people to be found in most societies. A very short time spent in a hostile foreign environment can teach one how vital diplomatic immunity is to the job, but it does nothing to make diplomats popular with the people they live among to see when diplomatic immunity is used to ignore parking tickets. Add to this diplomatic privileges (usually translated as duty-free booze) and "representation allowances," and the conclusions are obvious. Even if the perks can be justified, most fellow citizens would not see them as a natural right — although some FSOs certainly did.

The Treasury Board through its pre-auditor, a Mr Beech, saw things with microscopic clarity, and the value of the privileges accorded abroad were calculated with nicety and deducted from foreign service allowances. As for immunities, the Department itself let it be known that diplomatic immunity would be invoked only where official duties were involved except in countries where a fair trial could not be guaranteed.

Although the Department was the acknowledged interpreter and negotiator for Canada in the outside world, it had few programmes for which it was directly responsible: these were consular matters, passports and information abroad. Since most of the substance of foreign relations lay within the area of responsibility of other government departments, the Department was organized to see that the other departments concerned were always in the picture and that their points of view were understood and made a part of any foreign policy decision.

The assignment of responsibilities within the Department reflected the organization of responsibilities within the government as a whole. In addition to close and constant contact, the functional divisions of External (for instance, Economic or Defence Liaison) had client departments (Trade and Commerce, Finance, National Defence) whose interests they reflected within the Department.

The political or geographic divisions (for example, the European, or Africa and Middle East) were at the centre of the mainstream where diplomatic considerations proper (taking into account the totality of the relationships of the countries involved) held sway. Everything that went on in the geographical area under the eye of the political desk officer was his business and, if he could persuade the Head of his division that the issue was important enough, he could delay action by any other division or even any other department, at least until someone higher up in the hierarchy could rule on it.

The functional divisions represented the domestic realities and kept in close touch with the government departments that had primary responsibility in those areas. It was their job to see that the interests of the domestic departments were adequately considered within the Department on any given issue. If the department concerned did not have its way, it would have to know why. If it did not accept External's reasoning, the matter would very quickly rise to the deputy minister level and eventually, if necessary, it would go to cabinet for resolution.

As the functional divisions fought their clients' battles with the political divisions, the Department became the crucible in which Canadian domestic demands were mixed with the requirements of the outside world to become the amalgam called " diplomacy." There were also debates, and not just between divisions within the Department or between it and other departments with interests abroad to protect. Occasionally other departments would battle over issues in which External was not directly involved except as the executor of the policy that finally emerged: for example, a dispute between Trade and Commerce and National Defence about what constituted "military equipment" when potential enemies where the purchasers; or whether to open a new post abroad in a country with market potential rather than in one likely to remain an aid recipient.

There were harder ones. Trade negotiations such as those under the General Agreement on Tariffs and Trade presented particular problems sometimes involving conflicting regional interests within the country. The head of the Canadian delegation was usually an External official but with strong supporting talent from both Trade and Commerce and the Department of Finance. If, however, the head of delegation came from another department, External was able to insist that he should report not to his own department but through External.

Few internal disagreements became public. In the normal way of operating, it was the business of every department to resolve its own internal disputes. Disagreements between departments were usually settled by officials who knew that their ministers did not like being asked to confront their colleagues. Some ministers, it was thought, would sell the farm, so to speak, rather than take a disputed issue to cabinet. The result was that, whenever public servants could manage it, decisions were reached among officials in a non-stop series of interdepartmental negotiation that someone once described as a "floating crap game." It was a rare event when a minister refused to accept an agreement that had been reached by his officials; consequently, only a small proportion of these settlements ever went to cabinet. Very often a phone call between ministers or a few words before or after a cabinet meeting would produce a working agreement. If something more formal was required to record the understanding, it usually took the form of "Dear Colleague" letters between the ministers concerned. Once an issue went to cabinet, however, and a government policy was agreed, that was the end of it. No purpose would be served by making a public issue of it and certainly, in the forties and fifties, no public servant would have dreamed of appealing over the heads of ministers either to the public or to the Opposition.

The public servants who made this complex, and even subtle, system work effectively were a special breed, produced, no doubt, during the war when they would have been particularly conscious of the difference between their lot and that of those nearer the war. Public service was not a "right" but a privilege and, indeed, up until 1946, public servants were frequently chosen rather than hired on the open market.

For External there were additional qualifications and the Department's view of what constituted a generalist, or who would make a good FSO, was clearly revealed in the people it allowed (or invited) in. Although the bias in the forties and fifties was toward people who had done political science and economics (with a slight nod in favour of British universities), there were more classicists, political scientists and historians. The Department also boasted at least one physicist, one ex-clown and several published poets in both languages. Quite a few of these were could-be PhDs if they ever found time to finish their theses. Perhaps out of deference to these colleagues, FSOs who had doctorates never used the title. Later there were some FSOs who had actually studied international affairs but the Department wouldn't have given them any extra marks. The view was that if someone had a good academic record in just about any area and had shown in one way or another (eventually by examination) an ability to handle words and ideas, in writing and orally, the Department would teach him all he needed to know about international affairs.

The "University of the East Block" was an attempt to start this process of education for new FSOs. It began in the late forties. Attendance was not obligatory. The harried neophyte had walked into a job that was waiting for him and that was where his first obligation was. Most of the talks given were pragmatic: how the government was organized and how to do necessary things like finding a file. Some were on the organization of world politics, the new United Nations and the Commonwealth, for example. The lectures were usually given by Heads of Division.

The mysteries of "security" were cautiously revealed, but its twin sister, "intelligence," would be saved for later on. Diplomatic reporting was the most highly rated art and neophytes were exposed to it in the form of incoming telegrams and despatches from the moment they were provided with an "In" basket. Later the point would be made that diplomatic reporting and intelligence were really the same thing, only the sources were sometimes a bit different. Downplaying the importance of intelligence was elementary security. To romanticize intelligence would only draw attention to its existence. It was much wiser to encourage the view that it was nothing very special. Still later in the career there would be indoctrination into "special sources" and with it an introduction into a fascinating world whose very existence could not be shared with those who were not similarly indoctrinated.

On the security side there were rules about locking papers up and some hints about the lengths to which some people would go to find out what the Department was up to. There was some scoffing at all this but Igor Gouzenko had recently persuaded most doubters that there really were people who took an interest in the Department's activities. Telephones were viewed with particular suspicion. This was inhibiting in the days before scramblers were in common use, but all too often one said what one had to say on the phone and hoped for the best. Even Canadian negotiating positions were discussed during international telephone conversations in strange roundabout ways, for instance by referring to a government department by its location in Ottawa (Cartier Square for National Defence) or by the name of an assistant deputy minister, or a foreign country by the street in Ottawa where its embassy was located (Charlotte Street for Soviet Embassy). This wasn't likely to defeat even a mediocre intelligence agency, but it could delay most intelligence bureaucracies long enough to make the information useless. As time went on things got more sophisticated and the rules got stricter.

The course in the University of the East Block to "explain" the filing system was a noble effort in a lost cause. For many years, for instance, the Central Registry card index showed a file entitled "International Situation Generally." It contained one document, a prewar Foreign Office report relating to the prospects of war in the Balkans. Other files that had been opened to deal with a specific situation would become catch-alls for subjects only vaguely related to the listed title.

The Central Registry was a large room whose filing cabinets, stacked up to the high ceiling, were reached via an unpainted wooden scaffolding, a typical example of wartime expansion and improvisation. One soon learned that the way to get a file was to tell Mrs Hyde-Clarke, the presiding genius of the CR, what you were looking for. She would narrow down the choices and then either find the document or tell you who had the file. Desk officers rapidly learned that the only way to be sure of having the papers you needed to do your job was to keep your own files. When a desk officer left the job, which happened every year or so, he would normally leave his collection to his successor. Until the arrival of copy machines decades later, carbons (often barely legible) were kept of everything one produced and copies of the more important incoming papers were either lifted out of circulation or reproduced by a friendly typist.

The ability to express oneself concisely and lucidly, particularly on paper, was greatly admired by those who mattered in the Department. There was, for instance, the case of Douglas LePan, now best known as a poet. A graduate in English literature from the universities of Toronto, Oxford and Harvard, he joined the Canadian Army as a gunner and served until the war ended. In 1945, External sought him out, secured his discharge from the army and appointed him to the High Commissioner's Office in London.

According to the mythology of the time, on one occasion Canada House was invited to have someone attend a lecture to be given by the great economist John Maynard Keynes. More appropriate members of the staff were otherwise engaged and, not to leave the chair reserved for Canada empty, LePan was asked to go. In the normal way, he wrote a report on what the great man had said. The report so impressed LePan's High Commissioner that not only was it sent off to Ottawa but a copy was given to someone in the Foreign Office and, so the story goes, a further copy found its way back to Keynes himself. Lord Keynes did not normally take kindly to those who commented on his work, so when word trickled back to the Department that the great man had been favourably impressed by LePan's report, it was enough to put the author on the path to becoming, as he soon did, the Department's leading economic expert.

This story may well be apocryphal but the fact that it gained wide currency in External carried a message: if you are bright, flexible and able to write well, specialist expertise can be managed. And it is a fact that LePan, whose academic speciality was English literature, did become head of the Economic Division.

LePan was one of those rising stars who actually chose to leave Elysium to return to earth—in his case, the University of Toronto. His colleagues found the move hard to understand. Here was a person in the mainstream, a generalist *par excellence* of an institution that had effective control over the management of the foreign policy of the prototypical Middle Power, during a self-consciously Golden Age. How could he choose to give that up?

Such was the opinion that FSOs had of the Department and, of course, of themselves. This high self-esteem produced some strange reactions among those who worked in External. For instance there was an Ambassador, who had been head of post more than once, who became famous for his injudicious utterances. His final posting was to a country which, though democratic in form, had a spotty record in some of the niceties of human rights. On one occasion our man sent a despatch to Ottawa recounting in detail how, at a diplomatic reception, he had "beckoned the Prime Minister into a quiet nook" and there told him that the government of Canada took a very poor view of his host government's latest violation of democratic norms. (The PM had removed a political rival.) Our man reported that he had, on behalf of the Canadian government, ventured to hope that the Prime Minister wouldn't do that sort of thing any more.

In that era, when such things were considered a country's internal affairs and nobody else's business, our government had never expressed any such opinions, even to itself, and certainly it had never instructed the Ambassador to say what he had said. A letter was composed in the Department which began with a paragraph of faint praise for past services and a perfunctory appreciation of his embassy's reporting on the local scene. It then went on for three or four paragraphs telling the offending Ambassador very precisely why he should not have said what he had to the prime minister of his host country.

In due course, the Ambassador replied. He was most grateful for the Department's communication. It was very reassuring to know that his reports were read with interest and that his efforts were appreciated. Full stop. No one ever knew if he had read beyond the first paragraph and understood that he'd been dressed down or if he had just decided to ignore it.

At the other end of the spectrum were the "high fliers," as particularly promising young people were known in personnel circles. Some of them knew they were particularly promising young people; others may have known it but managed to conceal the fact; some went on to fulfil their promise while others just kept on being promising. In this group there was one otherwise worldly man who simply couldn't descend to the intellectual level at which, for instance, secret policemen operated. He was sent to open a post in a semi-friendly country and in due course he received his essential piece of equipment, the Taylor safe—very effective protection for cipher material and other highly sensitive documents. When it arrived, one of its two dials had been damaged and it was impossible to work the combination, which had been sent along by diplomatic bag. The bright young man telegraphed the Department to report this fact but before any response could be made, a second telegram arrived from him saying that all was well. He reported that, thanks to the foreign ministry, the safe had been repaired and was working satisfactorily. Departmental security dryly noted that it had probably been repaired by the same people who had damaged it in the first place, and they would have fixed it so they, too, could open it at will. The safe, net weight one ton, was shipped back to Ottawa. The effect the incident had on the individual concerned no doubt remained with him to the end of an undistinguished career.

Who got promoted and why was watched over more carefully by the employees than by the Department. One FSO kept minute records of all his contemporaries and near-contemporaries and could, on demand, provide faster and more accurate information than Personnel Division could (or would) on, for instance, the time-lapse between promotions for anyone on his list. In the forties and fifties, FSOs either got a promotion or didn't and there was no formal way of doing anything about it. The promotion process required that the files of all eligible persons be reviewed for each round of promotions. Even though Personnel's filing system was no better than that of the Central Registry, it never produced any widely accepted accusations of unfairness before formal grievance procedures were put in place in the late sixties. Assessments were made by one's bosses and reviewed by their bosses. The problems that did emerge from the system had more to do with inflation than under-appreciation, so that later on drastic measures had to be taken to keep the ability to walk on water from becoming a normal job requirement.

Promotion was not the only indicator of progress. There was equally intense and usually unavowed competition for particular jobs as they came up. In Ottawa, political divisions (the mainstream again) were first on the list of where people wanted to work. Currently active desks were also highly sought after, but for the junior FSO, it also mattered who would be your boss. There were favoured people to work for and there were the reverse. Even an unappealing job could become desirable if it meant working under one of the fancied chiefs. And, vice versa, no matter how interesting a job might be, if the boss was disliked the job went begging, at least to the extent that junior FSOs were able to choose. This also had its effect on the careers of the chiefs, once it became known that the younger members were avoiding one individual. A one-time high flier could find himself left abroad because he was considered to be an uncongenial colleague or a person no one wanted to work for.

Then there was the choice of posts. There were good solid grounds for the cynical view often expressed that if you wanted to go to Paris, study Chinese. Being posted to a country after working on its desk in the Department was unusual. People were regularly asked to put their choice of postings on record. The safe thing was to list Paris, London, Washington and New York first; it probably wouldn't get you posted there, but then at least you could complain if you were sent to Jakarta and found you didn't like it.

Generally speaking, European posts were preferred to the more exotic but out-of-the-way capital cities that were coming on stream in ever greater numbers. There was a good supply of people who felt a sense of mission and perhaps a challenge about going to such places and it is a tribute to the recruit selection process that there was never any shortage of people happy to go to Lagos or Dhaka — although those who were actually sent were not always the same people who had volunteered for them. People who actually asked for difficult posts could be treated with the same disdain as those who opted for the best.

In the Department at home, it was regarded as a backhanded compliment for an FSO to be placed in charge of one of the administrative operations. A job in Personnel Division, for instance, not only ensured for you the respect of your peers, it also meant that your file was never lost, even though FSOs working in Personnel were not promoted while on that job. When your tour was over, a reward for faithful service could be expected in the form of a good posting. The rule was that after about three years on a job in Ottawa, one could expect to be posted; and after three years abroad, except for heads of posts, FSOs could expect to come home, certainly after the first posting abroad. Cross-postings were not always a good sign, and as one ascended the ladder the most flattering posting of all was to Ottawa.

The ultimate career aspirations for a young moderately ambitious FSO in the fifties would be to head a division, preferably a political one, then to head a small embassy abroad. There should be no quibbling about first postings. The Department was entitled to one argument-free posting for a new FSO and later to have a relatively free hand in deciding where a person lucky enough to become an Ambassador should be sent for his first job as head of mission. After that there would be some lateral moves in the Department and abroad until, toward the end, perhaps a nice comfortable post abroad as a *belle fin de la carrière;* the embassy in Copenhagen, for instance, the "small but costly crown" that Leslie Chance, the original and durable head of the Consular Division, wanted but never got.

The persons of influence in the Department in the fifties and sixties were the assistant undersecretaries. They were extensions of the Undersecretary, the civil servant head of the Department and, through the Secretary of State for External Affairs, the Department's link with the government of the day. The Undersecretary had the right to choose those with whom he wished to share his job. Personal compatibility with himself and the other members of his team was a prime consideration.

Among the competitive bunch who staffed the Department, it was very important to give credit where credit was due and disastrous to take it for your own. Some managed better than others, but generosity was what made working in the Department the delight it was, in spite of long hours and exacting demands on one's personal life.

There could be few workplaces in which a boss was more important than in a diplomatic mission abroad. In other jobs, when the day's work was done you could go home and curse the s.o.b., seek consolation from your family and go back the next day to face the ogre refreshed. This did not happen on a diplomatic post, especially at a time when not only the younger diplomat himself but his wife as well were expected to perform services, after office hours and quite often of a semi-personal nature, for the head of mission and, indeed, for his wife as well. Greeting the Ambassador's guests at the door and taking their coats, passing drinks for him, opening and closing doors were part of the job. And when these jobs were done there were some posts where telling your spouse how you felt about your boss might be exploitable by the secret police.

On the other hand, the circumstances of living as part of a diplomatic mission could be extremely rewarding. Mutual support in difficult circumstances could have the effect of binding people together in something close to a family relationship — sometimes excessively so. There was the well-known occasion when an Ambassador, after approving local leave for his diplomatic secretary and his new wife, then insisted that his own wife go with them. The FSO escaped by cancelling his leave.

Diplomatic privileges in most countries were administered in the name of the head of post. Normally, other members got their diplomatic supplies, including booze, through him. This was usually a mere formality, but one Ambassador with teetotal tendencies made his underlings justify their demands for liquor by listing the entertainments they were planning before he would sign the required release. It wasn't good enough to say you liked to drink the stuff yourself.

No wonder there was a saying among younger FSOs that there were no such things as good posts or bad posts, only good heads of mission and bad heads of mission. Although some heads of mission could overplay the role of father figure, most would take on the personal troubles of a junior colleague in ways they wouldn't at home.

Obviously, the Foreign Service presented particular problems in the area of personnel selection and not all of the challenges were successfully met. Nor was the Department immune to the Peter Principle. At a time when the Department was expanding rapidly, there were people who were promoted beyond their level of competence. Some eventually found jobs they could do in the Department and went on doing them very well. Some hung on and continued to make difficulties for the personnel people, some opted out and went elsewhere, but very few were successfully fired. An organization with as good an opinion of itself as the Department could be expected to have special difficulty in dealing with its own mistakes. From time to time attempts were made to get rid of some FSOs after they'd been confirmed in their job and perhaps promoted more than once. The rules that protect the public service from politically motivated dismissals made it virtually impossible for the Department to get rid of people in these circumstances. It was hard to argue that the last promotion was a mistake or that someone who had just completed a tour as Ambassador was no longer useful. In the end, although life could be made uncomfortable for non-performers and retirement made to look pretty attractive, direct firing was rarely considered for mere incompetence, beyond the first year or so of service.

In a business that positively invites pomposity, a sense of humour can be the thing that sets a person apart. Marcel Cadieux, Head of Personnel, Undersecretary and Ambassador to Washington, did not suffer fools gladly but he had a glorious sense of humour. Although he sometimes looked like a lugubrious undertaker, he is remembered for his sharp tongue and even sharper mind. A true but unusual product of postwar External, he strove constantly to maintain professional standards and perform that miracle of combining obedience to political direction without compromising professional integrity. Marcel was a forceful influence on the Department in many ways and in many capacities from the early forties to the late seventies. He was a thorn in the side for some people, including ministers and even a prime minister, but he was absolutely convinced of the role External Affairs should play in government. Fiercely loyal to his concept of Canada, he was intolerant of those who were prepared to compromise on matters he considered non-negotiable. He could launch a diatribe against one of his favourite *bêtes noires* that would leave a listener paralysed with laughter and never once crack a smile himself. He knew little or no English when he joined the public service but soon had become a master of clear, accented but incisive English.

During the sixties Quebec functionaries tried to establish the province as an international entity and generally do end runs around Ottawa in matters relating to foreign affairs. Instructions were sent out informing Canadian missions abroad that when they received requests from Quebec representatives for assistance they should advise the enquirer to put the request through Ottawa. One anglophone Ambassador who had chosen to give his own liberal interpretation to these instructions arrived in Ottawa for a visit. As was his custom, Marcel invited him to lunch at the old Rideau Club. The subject of Quebec's activities abroad came up. The Ambassador mentioned an occasion on which he had acted contrary to the literal word of his instructions. He had been asked by a Quebec representative, who also happened to be an old friend, to arrange some meetings with local business people, a chore regularly performed by embassies for any Canadian interest. The Ambassador said he couldn't bring himself to refuse such a simple and routine request. Marcel listened patiently until the Ambassador had finished. He put down his knife and fork, leaned across the narrow table and snarled, "You like your job?" The point made, the conversation turned to other things. His departure from the Undersecretary's office for the Embassy in Washington in 1969 coincided with the beginning of the transformation of the Department in ways that few people in it, and fewer outside it, understood at the time. More of this later.

When Cadieux went to Washington it was to replace Ed Ritchie who, in turn, replaced him as Undersecretary. The game of musical chairs, sometimes involving London and New York as well, had been played several times in the postwar era involving Mike Pearson, Hume Wrong, Norman Robertson and Charles Ritchie. Ed had succeeded Charles in Washington. They are not related, but one Ritchie following another saved the taxpayer the cost of printing new invitation cards for "The Ambassador of Canada and Mrs Ritchie."

Charles Ritchie is probably the best known departmental figure of them all. His career spanned the Golden Age and went well into the less gilded days that followed. For an entire generation of FSOs, he was the personification of what a Canadian diplomat could be, and successive governments acknowledged his pre-eminence in the trade by the use they made of him. He is the only person who has been at one time or another High Commissioner in London, Ambassador in Washington, to the United Nations, to Nato and in Bonn. The only significant job in the Department he never held full-time was the Undersecretary's and that may well have been his choice. His writing is well known to Canadians. The departmental records will eventually provide more examples of his lucidity and wit when they are finally opened to public scrutiny.

The stories about Charles Ritchie that have circulated in the Department are legion. They form a mythology of their own but they all have a single characteristic. A naïve, accident-prone, uncomplicated Nova Scotian finds himself in a situation he does not quite appear to understand. Then it suddenly seems that he really did understand, better than those around him. The first part of the portrait is Ritchie's own doing. As a listener in a profession where such people were rare, politicians and other diplomats, even journalists, confided in him because he was more concerned to understand what he was being told than to impress his informant with his own vast knowledge of the subject.

The Department of the fifties had two main types of heads of post: the professional and the political appointee. There was a smaller third category, of assimilated academics such as George Glazebrook and Bert MacKay, both practising university professors who became as much a part of the professional scene as any who had worked their way up from the bottom. The strictly political appointees were bound to be much more of a mixed bag considering that the reason for their selection usually had little to do with the needs of the Department and everything to do with the desires of the government.

When the war was over, there was a sudden need for people to head the new diplomatic missions that had to be opened at once. Promotion was rapid within the Department and a surprising number of people were found in the Foreign Services of External and Trade and Commerce to keep the show on the road, but inevitably others had to be brought in from somewhere. The government drew on a variety of sources: the law, academe, politics, business, other branches of the public service and the armed forces. Although all heads of mission are necessarily appointed by Order in Council (i.e., by cabinet), those with a known political connection or whose selection was motivated by political considerations were called "political." However, if they survived more than one posting, they were usually accepted as full members of the Department. Some very political individuals fitted in so well that the Department was glad to accept them as its own. Others carried the political appointee label to the end.

Lieutenant-General Maurice Pope, for instance, was a professional in a sense. His background was much more military than diplomatic but as Mackenzie King's military secretary through much of the war he was well versed in the ways of the Ottawa bureaucracy. He was also a son of the Department's first Undersecretary, Sir Joseph Pope. His appointment to the Military Mission in Berlin, the antecedent of the Canadian Embassy to the Federal Republic of Germany, was a logical one. He then went on to serve as Canadian Ambassador in Brussels. It would be difficult to categorize him as a "pol," but he did not fit into the FSO mould either.

The Honourable T.C. Davis, by any standard, was indisputably political. He had represented Mackenzie King's federal constituency of Prince Albert in the Saskatchewan legislature and had kept the seat safe for the Prime Minister as long as he was there. It was only after his departure that the constituency was lost by the Liberal Party (to a Conservative named John Diefenbaker) and the Prime Minister had to seek a seat elsewhere. Toward the end of the war Davis was made High Commissioner to Australia, an important post in terms of the war effort. From there he went to Nanking as Ambassador to Nationalist China. He left that post as the Red Army under Mao entered the southern capital and it was he who made the decision not to follow the Nationalist government to Taiwan. Later he became Ambassador in Bonn and in Tokyo. Although his personality had little in common with most of the FSOs who worked for him, he was generally liked by them and they by him. Tommy Davis brought with him the politician's ease in making friends, particularly among politicians in the countries in which he was posted.

T.C. Davis illustrates the ways in which the diplomat and the politician resemble each other. They deal with the same material, the diplomat as an observer, the politician as a practitioner. In both professions much of their success depends on an ability to get along with people. Consequently the transition from politics to diplomacy wasn't too difficult for good politicians. From the point of view of the Foreign Service, the political appointees who created problems were those who had been presented to the Department because they had not been very good at their previous job. On the other hand, many former politicians served the country well in the Department after their retirement from politics. Vincent Massey, George Drew, Paul Martin and Gérard Pelletier, for instance, all made their contributions to Canadian diplomacy.

In a small institution as the Department was during the forties and fifties (1,350 at home and abroad in 1950, compared to nearly 9,000 in 1990), everyone knew everyone else at least by reputation. Most problems could be handled in a personal way or anticipated and avoided more easily than in a larger organization where formalities and channels of communication had to be taken into account. External was continuing to operate on a personal basis — perhaps after it became inefficient to do so — and no doubt it must have seemed off-hand or unfair to those who were unfamiliar with its ways. In any event, as the Department grew, the easy informality gave way to more bureaucratic attitudes. But while it lasted, it had a spirit, an atmosphere and people that all combined to serve the country's interests effectively. It was also a wonderful place to work.

2

The Middle Power Model

If External Affairs was a wonderful place to work in the forties and early fifties, Ottawa was not much of a city to live in. The most imposing structures were the Parliament Buildings, while the Chateau Laurier and its pale imitator, the Lord Elgin, were the only hotels of any consequence. But it was a compact place where it was possible to come to know everyone who mattered, at least on a nodding basis. Mr St. Laurent as Prime Minister, like Mr King before him, went to national day receptions at foreign embassies (or legations, which still existed and were more common). He also walked three or four blocks to work, up Elgin Street from the Roxborough Apartments to the East Block. Men doffed their homburgs as they passed, and he doffed back.

In spite of the relaxed atmosphere, Ottawa was in an intellectual ferment and had been ever since 1944 when it became apparent that a victorious end to the war might be deferred but would not be denied. There were the enormous problems of demobilizing over a million men and women then in the three armed services, retooling for peaceful purposes an economy that had performed prodigies in military production, and launching a social welfare programme that is still largely in place. Externally, the challenges were at least as great. During the war years, Canada had moved beyond the point where it could allow the United Kingdom to play a prominent part in the conduct of its foreign operations. This had continued to be the practice in spite of the great increases in Canada's international activities and the almost explosive expansion in its international representation that took place as the war ended. In 1945 one officer in the High Commissioner's Office in London was accredited as chargé d'affaires to some seven governments in exile. As these governments returned to their own national capitals, the choice for Canada was either to open diplomatic missions or cease having relations with countries such as France, Belgium, the Netherlands, Norway and Denmark.

Even more important than Canada's material expansion was the expansion of roles and functions. Canada had discovered that it had its own unique interests abroad, or at least that it had interests that were shared only by smaller countries like itself. It also learned that war presented special threats, not because Canada had suffered in ways that could compare with the traumas of France, Germany or the USSR, but because war divided the country internally and disrupted its foreign trade–based economy.

Canada required an international system that could prevent war. For this purpose and for the sake of protecting its new international interests, its government wanted a role in the international community that matched the country's newly discovered ability to "contribute." And "contribute" was an "in" word in the Ottawa of the late forties. Democratic equality among states was obviously impossible, but at least the system should reflect the functional powers of the less-than-great: their ability to contribute.

The international system, the world order from time immemorial, had been based on relations between the Great Powers, usually shortened to "the Powers," which ordered the affairs of the world to suit their convenience. Usually this system precluded war, which was ordinarily viewed by the Powers as an interruption of the business of self-enrichment. War, when it came, was the result of a threat to the status quo by one of the Powers wanting more territory, commerce or simply prestige.

In the international system that applied up to 1945, at least, the less-than-great made their way in the world under the protection of one or another of the Powers and paid for the service by offering their patron some strategic advantage such as strategic bases, raw materials or manpower. When the war ended in 1945 the Powers that emerged, if not intact, then at least on the winning side, saw no reason for changing the old, familiar system. Consequently, the Charter of the United Nations reasserted the old rules in giving the Powers that were on the winning side permanent seats on the Security Council and the right to veto its substantive decisions.

Very soon after the end of the war in Europe, Canada showed signs of rebelling against the assumption (and not just in the UN) that the Powers would make the decisions and the less-than-great would decide how best to conform to them. Instead, it sought Great Power recognition that there were countries that did not have the near-universal interests of a Great Power but which were "great" for some purposes and in some regions. When these functions and regions were being considered, it was argued these Middle Powers should be consulted. In pushing the concept Canadians made common cause with other members of the Commonwealth — Australia, New Zealand, South Africa and occasionally India — and, particularly, with the Scandinavians.

The idea of the Middle Power, if not invented in Canada, should have been. It became External's job, in concert with "like-minded countries," to have the concept accepted within the international community. This was not a separate agenda item but a philosophical outlook that was built into the government's position on whatever issue happened to be at hand. It was in this process of reworking the system while using it that the Department of External Affairs helped to move Canada into a position in the outside world that was out of all proportion to the country's relative importance.

The concatenation of circumstances that enabled Canada to have its way to the extent it did has been described many times. France was demoralized and momentarily humiliated. Italy, freed of its fascist pretensions, had been deflated to something like its actual size. Germany had been flattened, Japan simply beaten. China was in chaos and Britain had all but ruined itself in the process of winning. On this flat landscape Canada was a conspicuous landmark of stability, even prosperity, comparable only to the United States itself. Its reputation had reached inside the barbed wire of the Auschwitz concentration camp where the food storehouse was labelled "Kanada." But this postwar pre-eminence was a temporary state of affairs and it was recognized as such within the Department.

Canadian negotiators from External as well as from Finance, Trade and Commerce and the Bank of Canada made the most of this transitory position in the hectic rounds of negotiations that rewrote the book on international economic relationships during the first decade after the war. Canadian diplomatists were active not only at Bretton Woods, where the World Bank and the International Monetary Fund began, but in San Francisco where the United Nations Charter was hammered out. A little later they took an active part in the drafting of the North Atlantic Treaty where they showed that Canada's UN-based idealism did not blind it to the realities of the deepening Cold War. Some of these same people represented Canada in the creation of the Colombo Plan in 1950 when Third World development first appeared on the agenda of industrialized countries.

It has been claimed (or alleged) that Nato was originally a Canadian idea. Regardless of who first thought of it, the fact is that the

North Atlantic Treaty perfectly suited Canada's overwhelming desire never again to be torn between its European roots and its North American location. The effects of being at war while the United States was neutral between 1939 and 1941 had been especially hard on Canada. Moreover, it was the conventional wisdom of the time that Nazi aggression had been made possible by American neutralism. Canada therefore had its own particular interest in wanting to see American and European defences linked. It is a measure of Canada's influence at the time that it was able to have an economic clause inserted in the text of the North Atlantic Treaty in spite of Great Power objections. It does not matter that the provisions failed to give Nato a non-military dimension, as Pearson (who had them inserted) had hoped they would; the point is that Canada had the skill and influence to get its way.

External's postwar "Greats" — the Pearsons, the Robertsons, the Wrongs, the Ritchies, the Reids and the Riddells — went to these world-shaping conferences well prepared. They were armed with information and expertise to a degree that was not normal at a time when free-wheeling amateurism was still a diplomatic norm. Canadian delegations acquired a reputation for doing their homework and, through the use of such unusual, not to say unfair, tactics, were able to influence decisions well beyond what was considered normal for a non-Great Power. The leaders of these bands of happy warriors were more than willing to give credit to their supporting team, the likes of John Holmes, Marcel Cadieux, Jack Pickersgill, Ed Ritchie, Tommy Stone, Saul Rae, George Ignatieff. This last group were not only allowed to carry the briefing bags of the others, they also helped to fill them with ammunition and sometimes to use it in the innumerable subcommittees where so much of the duelling took place in these conferences.

Along with the search for the prize of Middle Powership, there was another tendency that had spread rapidly under the pressure of war. It was what in retrospect could be called Canadian nationalism, although that would not have been a term any of the External Greats would have lightly used. Its most visible sign was a gradual but steady removal of the British leading strings. British tutelage had been an issue for the Canadian armed forces during the war when it was resented but accepted in the interests of getting on with the fight. However, once the war was over, the British connection, which had served Canada's interests well in a world run by the Powers, began to be de-emphasized. At first, British policy guidance was looked at carefully and perhaps even followed, other things being equal. Later, as the government acquired its own sources of information, the influence lessened. At the same time British diplomatic practices and attitudes that sometimes made Canada look very British to casual European and American observers gradually began to be phased out. The situation also led to some confusion. In the US State Department, Canadian relations were handled by those responsible for European affairs, while in some European foreign ministries responsibility for Canada was moving from sections dealing with the British Empire to sections dealing with the United States.

Disengagement from the British sphere of influence was a gradual and delicate process. Canada continued for some time to depend heavily on British facilities and expertise. Although the government wanted to establish Canada's independence from Britain in the minds of third parties, it was important not to cut off the absolutely essential technical and practical help the British were still so generously providing, particularly in the many areas of the world where we had no representation of our own. Into the sixties, many of our missions abroad were serviced by British diplomatic couriers. In the field of intelligence and security we imported British experts like Peter Dwyer, who later came in out of the cold to become the first head of the Canada Council. Consequently, in matters of security and intelligence, as in other areas, we went on doing things in the British way long after we stopped depending on London.

The movement out from under British patronage was well under way by the mid-fifties and, oddly enough, it was led by people who had had close personal links with the United Kingdom, usually in the form of a British university education — Oxford, Cambridge and the London School of Economics preferred. This may have helped ensure that within the Department the movement away from British models never amounted to a total rejection (and certainly not of British help). It was seen, probably by the British as well, to be a necessary consequence of our struggle for our own place in the world. Partly, too, it would have been a response to French-Canadian scorn for the unabashed colonial who still flourished in some segments of English Canada.

A case in point. In the wake of the 1946 Report of the Royal Commission into the Gouzenko affair, the House of Commons voted to unseat one of its members, Fred Rose, the only Communist ever to sit there and one of the people who had been exposed by the Gouzenko papers. Those supporting Rose's expulsion claimed that he was unworthy of membership in the House because he had shown himself to have had "a higher allegiance to another country." During the debate Jean-François Pouliot, the *enfant terrible* of the Liberal government benches, declared that if giving prior allegiance to another country was grounds for removing a member of Parliament, then the honourable member for Rosedale — Thomas Church, a high Tory when there were such things — should also be removed for the same reason. One of Mr Church's recurrent themes was that Canada didn't really need a Department of External Affairs since the British Foreign Office was available and did a much better job.

Not everyone who supported the gradual movement away from Britain did so without reservations. J.L. Granatstein in *The Ottawa Men* quotes Escott Reid, the Department's best known "futurist," writing as early as 1943 on the Canadian need for a military security system. In his view Canadians "have not won from London complete freedom to make our own decisions on every issue — including that of peace and war — in order to become a colony of Washington. It would thus appear probable that effective military cooperation between Canada and the United States is possible only within the framework of an effective world order in which both Canada and the United States are loyal members."

Wariness of "the Americans" has been a constant in Canadian political thinking since 1776 if not before. While Canadian and American individuals made their own arrangements across the frontier, the standard Canadian government position was to avoid areas of known US sensitivity. These areas included, particularly, matters remotely connected to US national security and sometimes issues involving what was termed "discrimination," when American-owned interests in Canada were treated less favourably than Canadian-owned equivalents. The normal Canadian posture was to be noncommittal on matters of principle and deal with American complaints each on its own merits, never across the board. In spite of this wariness, however, the movement away from London did lead the Department to look more to Washington for ideas, information and leadership than had been the case before the war.

For their part the British, preoccupied with other problems, accepted the distancing of Canada philosophically. They were, after all, busy sloughing off the trappings of Empire and were themselves working on a special relationship with the United States. The speed with which Canada shifted from British to American models (in the military field, for instance) has meant the loss to Canada of some useful cultural counterweights.

In spite of the government's best efforts to emphasize Canada's independence in the postwar world, old ideas died hard in the international community. Well into the sixties an uncertainty persisted in many countries about our relations with both Britain and the United States. Here again the establishment of Canada as the prototype Middle Power was a great help. Canada's new description suited it well geographically, politically and temperamentally, while at the same time making it easier to distinguish Canadian positions from those of both Britain and the United States. The policies it adopted internationally further strengthened the distinction.

In the years immediately following the war, the Department had perfected its own brand of Middle Power diplomacy based on doing its homework and looking for compromises, preferably in the positions adopted by others but inevitably in matters affecting its own interests as well. Ideological positions, even positions on principle, were talked about but seldom allowed to become a breaking point in negotiation. When other countries were staking out their maximum demands in a negotiation, the Canadian delegation was looking for middle ground which, it often happened, would also serve Canada's own interests.

Nevertheless, it was not a time of unalloyed success for Canadian diplomacy. The UN Charter, for instance, left the new organization weaker than Canada would have had it. But a new arrival in the Department in the late forties or early fifties could have no doubt that he was joining an institution that was both high-minded and effective. The diplomacy it conducted was serving the country's interests well and had given Canada an identifiable international personality: not myopically selfish, apparently naïve, self-consciously responsible, open-minded on almost any subject, painfully self-righteous, constitutionally mysterious and withal, rather well-to-do.

Throughout this time the Department had few operational responsibilities of its own; virtually all the submissions it made to cabinet affected the responsibilities of other departments and had been pre-negotiated with them. Very often the result was a joint submission signed by more than one minister. Briefing papers for a session of the United Nations General Assembly, depending on the agenda, contained material provided by Trade and Commerce, Citizenship and Immigration, the Wheat Board, Fisheries, Agriculture, the Secretary of State or National Defence as well as External itself. Consultation was the name of External's game, especially where future commitments were concerned. There must be no surprises.

The Department of the time saw itself as a collection of all-round men (and a few extra-good women) who could take on board enough information in any area to be able to deal with any issue that might arise in any international gathering, be it the UN Security Council or the Commonwealth War Graves Commission. Specialists were available for consultation and they were content to leave the mechanics of international negotiation to External.

The decade that followed the war was a time when new international organizations were created to deal with new issues on the international scene. Beginning with the UN itself and its principal organs and specialized agencies, negotiating forums like the International Monetary Fund, the General Agreement on Tariffs and Trade, the International Atomic Energy Agency, the UN Educational, Scientific and Cultural Organization were all created by negotiations in which Canada participated fully. Once created, these organizations all held meetings that had to be attended. It was a matter of course that Canadian delegations should be present, well briefed and active.

In each case a decision had to be made about the part to be played by the experts in the subject. There was no question on the leadership. The head of delegation was either from External or, if he was from another department, under instructions to report through External. The Department's starting position was that in most of these negotiations a knowledge of the rules that governed such gatherings and of Canada's other international commitments that might be affected would be paramount. This placed a heavy burden on the Externalite with no background in science who had been chosen to lead a delegation negotiating, say, the terms of an agreement to limit the spread of nuclear technology. But it left the experts free to do the in-fighting in the subcommittees where the substantive work was done.

The Department's view on this was widely accepted; if specialists were allowed to roam the world making decisions based solely on the interests of their speciality, the agreements they negotiated would not only conflict with each other, they would also cut across other broader interests to which the government, and often the public, attached even more importance. Promoting the sale of nuclear products could conflict with our Non-Proliferation Treaty obligations, trading with Cuba conflicted with our desire to maintain good relations with the United States and the exchange of military intelligence among allies could conflict with the role of the peacekeeper. If there had been no body, with no special interests of its own, available to look at the total effect of individual actions taken on behalf of the country, there would have been gaps and overlaps in our diplomatic defences that other countries could exploit. Someone must be responsible for looking after the interests of the country as a whole and over the longer term. For two decades the Department was able to insist that it and it alone should have that responsibility and that, unless the Secretary of State for External Affairs played a central part in all negotiations in all areas, he could not be held responsible to Parliament for the whole picture.

Ministers, including prime ministers from King through St. Laurent, Diefenbaker and Pearson, accepted this view and usually gave External the support it needed to override, when it came down to that, powerful sectoral interests represented in the government. The export of arms and other strategic materials, for instance, was legally under the control of the Minister of Trade and Commerce in consultation with the Secretary of State for External Affairs. Although there were pressures to alter established government policy to meet some specific commercial interest, it was rarely done. On the other hand, as should be expected in a country as dependent on international trade as Canada, commercial interests were given enormous weight during the development of new policies.

Thus, the Department's role from the end of the war until 1968 was that of a secretariat whose main function was to watch over and negotiate on behalf of all of Canada's interests abroad. This was not always cheerfully accepted by the specialist departments, and External was obliged to spend a great deal of its time keeping its contacts with other departments in good working order through consultation before, during and after negotiation.

The closest relationship was with the Department of Trade and Commerce which, at the time, was the only other department to employ Foreign Service Officers. The relationship was not without its tensions, but it may not have been mere coincidence that while External was having its Golden Age in the field of diplomacy, the Trade Commissioner Service was enjoying worldwide recognition for providing Canadian business with better support abroad than was being offered by any other country.

In the late forties and early fifties that "floating crap game," the co-ordination of interdepartmental positions, went on daily all over Ottawa, very often in public. On almost any working day deputy ministers could be observed at lunch in the Chateau Laurier cafeteria, carrying their trays into quiet corners there where they would wheel and deal. More formal meetings on matters of foreign operations were normally sponsored or chaired by External, which also would provide the secretary who might later become the secretary of the negotiating delegation.

The process of consultation was consistent with External's operating assumption that it was the guardian of all of Canada's national interests abroad and the prime source of all international negotiating expertise. But there were exceptions. There were, for instance, acknowledged experts within both Trade and Commerce and Finance who regularly carried the main burden of trade and tariff negotiation. However, in general, they were happy to be rid of the formal and organizational part of international conferences and left free to pursue the black art of translating an import quota into a tariff concession.

All things considered, it would not be surprising if the staff of External Affairs in the late forties and early fifties knew that they had influence within the government; that the government would take their views about the outside world seriously. But they were also realists. They also knew there were limits beyond which they must not go. Nothing they proposed must threaten long-standing national interests. The Department should not propose anything that could damage Canada's ability to sell wheat (to the devil himself if possible); nothing it suggested should trespass on provincial rights (the Privy Council had ruled that the federal government could not invade provincial jurisdiction on the pretext of honouring an international commitment); nor should its ideas cost a great deal of money to implement. Otherwise External was not only free but encouraged to pursue the widely accepted view of Canada's destiny; first to help construct a world order that included a place for Middle Powers and then to play to the hilt the part it had helped to create.

Just as there were domestic reasons why Canadian diplomacy could not take a bee-line toward its objectives, there were at least equal inhibitions that originated in the outside world, chiefly in the United States. Before World War II was under way, the President of the United States had declared that the United States "would not stand idly by" if Canadian soil was threatened from without. The reciprocal statement by Mackenzie King was that Canada had an obligation to see that the United States was not attacked from across Canadian territory. Canada's ability to act independently in the foreign environment could never be permitted to reach the point where it might give rise to plausible American fears that their territorial security could be jeopardized by any act of a Canadian government.

During the postwar period, the Department and its ministers (first Louis St. Laurent and then Mike Pearson) enjoyed enough of the government's confidence that within the limitations mentioned, they were free to pursue the country's other external objectives without much intervention either from cabinet or Parliament. This combination of the circumstances of the time, the nature of the government, the personality of the ministers and the character of the Department became the basis of the External myth that still lingers. It is arguable that at no time since has Canada operated internationally with such assurance and independence.

The Korean War and Canada's involvement with it, as told by Pearson's biographer, John English, illustrate the influence External Affairs had on government policy. At this time of great tension, Canada was able to maintain a position that was significantly different from that of the United States on a major international issue while at the same time co-operating with it fully in the defence and restoration of the independence of South Korea.

Between 1950 and 1953, over the objections of a rapidly aging Mackenzie King, Canada helped resist the incursion of North Korea into South Korea. Even more important, when the Soviet Union walked out of the Security Council, Canada played a significant if not a decisive part in having the war waged as a police action of the United Nations. In this way, Canada participated in support of the United Nations rather than as a response to the urgent demands of the United States. This did not mean that Canada or the United Nations had much to say about how the war was conducted by its military commander, General Douglas MacArthur. Even the American government had problems in that regard. Nevertheless, the position taken by Canadian representatives in New York could leave no doubt that Canada was acting on its own responsibility as a Middle Power in a matter affecting world peace and security. Even given the Cold War it managed to act as a member of the United Nations rather than simply as an ally or protégé of a Great Power.

Keeping the balance between independence from the United States and alliance with it was a constant theme in Canada's international activity. In spite of this, the country's political independence was not as widely recognized as it might have been in the early fifties. The general public in other countries found it hard to categorize Canada. The British imperial connection — Canadian troops fought in a Commonwealth Brigade in Korea — and the proximity of the United States continued to affect the way Canada was viewed abroad. Nevertheless, the Department attached little importance to its own task of projecting a more accurate view of Canada's constitutional and international position. The innate reluctance to spend money applied particularly in the matter of Canadian information abroad, although this was one of the Department's few operational responsibilities. The tendency was to regard the information abroad programme as a matter of propaganda and not quite respectable.

As late as 1955, the Information Division was the orphan of the Department. Most of those who worked in the division, however, had a missionary's urge to tell all the world everything there was to tell about the country. The rest of External thought that particular goal was impossible — a bottomless pit — or, if possible, dangerously unwise. Like most diplomats, the Department's leaders regarded information in the way that bankers look at money; as something to acquire and to guard but to give away only if you could get more of it in return. Everybody acknowledged that the Department had an obligation to inform the Canadian public about matters of foreign policy but most would have preferred to have had it done through, say, the Canadian Institute for International Affairs (CIIA) through which External kept in touch with its most important constituents, the academic and journalistic communities. There was no comparable compulsion to satisfy the curiosity of the rest of the world.

The Information Division of External Affairs had been created shortly after the war by the absorption of what started as the Wartime Information Board and later became the Canadian Information Service. Most of its personnel were women who believed passionately in what they were doing. Canada had something to export to the rest of the world — politically, socially and, yes, culturally — and it was their privilege to get the product out.

The Department was uncertain about culture. At that time in all of Canada there were barely three symphony orchestras, not much theatre (Stratford was still a glint in Tom Patterson's eye), a small number of painters, a handful of authors with domestic reputations, and even fewer poets. Only the National Film Board had anything like an international reputation. To most people Canada was a heavy importer of culture with little to offer in return. Nevertheless, it was External's responsibility to see that the artistic community was represented on the world scene until the Canada Council took that job over in the late fifties to the general relief of all concerned.

Information on foreign policy was different. Apart from the CIIA, whose advice and assistance were often sought and frequently followed, not even federal politicians showed much interest in what the country was doing internationally. Foreign policy was an arcane subject that could be best discussed within the framework of a learned society. Few questions were asked in Parliament and as a rule there was only one debate a year on External Affairs, when the Department's estimates were brought down. That was an occasion for the government to boast a little while the Opposition, apparently reluctant to challenge the government in this area, muttered pious generalities.

Questions in the House of Commons, when they came, were usually asked by members who actually wanted information — but occasionally attempts were made to score points. For instance, in the late forties there were questions like this:

1. What is the name of the Ambassador to Godless Russia and what is his salary?
2. What is the name of the Ambassador to the Holy See and what is his salary?

MPs had no one to do their homework for them yet; their questions often went amiss. The answer to that particular sally was that there was no Ambassador to the USSR (there happened to be a chargé d'affaires in Moscow at the time) and none in the Vatican. Point lost.

The Information Division inevitably attracted some public attention, first among the members of the cultural community, and then among some astute members of the business community who saw more clearly than the government that information about Canada was a necessary part of their own export sales programmes. The division of labour for information abroad gave the Department of Trade and Commerce responsibility for the promotion of Canadian exports. External was supposed to do everything else, and it was not very effective so far as Canadian exporters were concerned. The result was a business-sponsored Committee on Information Abroad which met annually for many years at the Seigneury Club in Montebello. It was a ginger group which tried to push the Department into doing more to make Canada better known abroad as background for their more specific promotional advertising.

The Department was no better at generating information to support its own activities within the international community. The main reason was simply the magnitude of the task. Any serious attempt to "sell" Canada abroad would have dominated the Department's agenda (not to mention its budget) at a time when it had more important foreign policy objectives and it did not see any compelling connection between the two activities. One result of this view of "information work" was that Information Division had a new Head every two or three years, normally a rank amateur, an FSO who rarely stayed long enough to learn the business. This was consistent with the Department's opinion of experts and its view that any decent FSO should have no trouble running the sort of information programme the Department thought necessary.

Underlying these practical difficulties was a philosophical split on what Canada's information policy should be, had all the resources been available. On one side were those people, mostly in the Information Division, who would have liked to tell the world all there was to know about Canada. On the other side was virtually everyone else in the Department, who acknowledged an obligation to answer direct questions about the country but without stimulating further inquiries. This conflict applied with special effect in the United States where the policy was and remained entirely responsive. When a schoolteacher in Boise, Idaho, gave a class an assignment on Canada, both the Department and the Embassy in Washington were deluged with letters asking for information about "your wonderful country." The class got what it wanted, although all concerned knew that this was not the best use of resources.

The other possible approach was to promote, selectively but actively. In 1956 as a result of the direct involvement of Jules Léger, then Undersecretary, there was a co-ordinated effort by External and Trade and Commerce to see if the information programme in the United States could be improved. Inquiries in New York revealed what other countries were doing in the undisputed media centre of the United States. The British operation was beyond belief: subtle, effective and expensive. The answers were intimidating rather than inspiring and, except for specific efforts in limited areas, the responsive approach was continued.

For posts in the United States the approach to information raised a number of particularly difficult questions. Put in possibly oversimplified terms, the early view was that Americans should not be encouraged to know any more than they already knew about Canada.

American intentions toward Canada were considered at best ambivalent so it was assumed that the more the Americans knew about our exciting country, the more interested they might become in eliminating those artificial boundaries between us. Canadians had the advantage, it was assumed, of knowing all they needed to know about the United States, so why not just let the other side go on thinking that we were "just like them"? There were others who argued that we were burying our heads in the sand, that Canada was too important to the United States to hide and that it would be better for the Americans to get the facts of Canadian life from us rather than pick up their information, so to speak, in the gutter. Being taken for granted would one day prove dangerous and besides, the Americans that Canadian business leaders and officials dealt with were very well informed indeed. It would be better for everyone if the Americans at least knew how we saw ourselves.

The debate between the two viewpoints was largely academic since budgets would never permit more than a responsive information programme punctuated by the odd special campaign. However, even within the limitations of available resources, there were some obvious target groups, such as members of Congress. There was some rather daring discussion of the possibility of dealing with legislators in Congress directly instead of through the State Department as the rules said we should. In the end, it was agreed that there should be a new desk in the embassy to deal with congressional relations but that it was not to be called by that name — out of consideration for the State Department.

There were no dramatic results from the 1956 review of information practices, just an increase of two or three in the number of people doing information work in the United States. The debate between the "responsive" and the "promotional" schools was still going on when the argument was overtaken by the growth of the North American television networks. Popular culture became an industry standardized largely on American models and information became a market commodity with accuracy giving way to quantity. Misconceptions about Canada were not countered in the networks, they were propagated. The Department's response was a further concentration of effort on target groups (such as the financial leaders of New York) and specific subjects (such as the Canadian economy). Journalists were encouraged to travel the length and breadth of the country, university chairs on Canadian studies were encouraged and supported.

In every Golden Age there are bound to be bits of dross and certainly the information function was one area in which the Department did not exactly glitter. The very things that made External's analysts and negotiators so good at their jobs probably also made them contemptuous of the unseemly blowing of one's own horn that is "PR." It was not seen as having any relevance to the country's aspirations to Middle Power status. There was also something unethical about trying to make end-runs around a fellow foreign ministry by dealing directly with politicians or, worse, the people. External would certainly have resented comparable activities by the US Embassy in Ottawa, for instance, although under our system of government influencing individual MPs would have had less point than influencing a Congressman.

Ignorance about Canada was by no means confined to the United States. To an extent that was not widely realized at the time, the rest of the world saw Canada as a contradiction and an anomaly. People who were not familiar with our history — which was almost everyone — simply looked at a map. They saw a very artificial-looking dividing line separating this country from the most powerful state on earth. They might also have heard both Americans and Canadians call this line a "border," the word used to describe historical demarcation lines (between, say England and Scotland), rather than a "frontier," as divisions between sovereign states are usually called. On the other hand, in most atlases Canada was shown in pink along with other members of the not quite defunct British Empire. The result was that only people who knew the country quite well accepted Canada as a truly independent state.

In Europe in the early fifties any travelling Canadian could expect to have some variation of the following conversation:

Q. I understand you are a Canadian, but what is a Canadian? Are you an American or are you British?
A. Neither. Canada is an independent country.
Q. Yes, I know, but does that mean you are American?
A. No. I am a Canadian.
Q. Then you must be British.
A. No. I am a Canadian.
Q. I don't understand. You must be one or the other. (And so on)

Canada has never conformed to the European norms for nationality. The French in particular have always had difficulty in acknowledging Canada's real statehood since it failed to meet the Napoleonic norm of the nation-state: citizens bound together by common history, geography, language, culture and, often, religion. What foreigners see in their atlases and what they hear about the multinational state leads to questions and reservations.

Moreover, most Europeans, who know little of our history, wondered how that enormous piece of real estate, rich in resources, underpopulated and right up against the United States, could be truly independent. Even Americans, many of whom believe they won the War of 1812, must also wonder how Canada could be truly independent.

There may not have been much that could have been done in the 1950s to give the world a more accurate picture of Canada's position in it. The Department's point of view, as we have seen, was that the right place to make the point was through its conduct at international gatherings, by being a Middle Power, and not in propaganda activity. There was an exception.

By the mid-fifties the Cold War was well under way and Canada was in it, at least on the verbal front. Our principal contribution, with strong encouragement from our allies, was the International Service of the Canadian Broadcasting Corporation (CBCIS), then transmitting in several East European languages. Much of CBCIS's funding was provided through the Department but the broadcasts were entirely of the CBC's own making. Foreign listeners became puzzled to the point of writing letters when some commentator, whose remarks were often originally intended for the CBC national network, attacked some point of Canadian policy. Others were more than puzzled when the policies of allied countries were given the same sort of treatment, say in Russian, on shortwave. It was decided that CBCIS should have some guidance. It was argued that at the very least it should know what the government's policies were. Then the CBCIS could still say what it liked about those policies but the government's official position on any specific issue should be accurately reported in the process.

Arrangements were made for liaison between the Department and CBCIS, particularly with the producers and broadcasters responsible for the various language programmes intended for "the other side." Nothing as crude as prior censorship was suggested. After programmes had been broadcast, External was given copies of the scripts that had been used by commentators. These were read with the idea of drawing attention to instances in which Canadian policy had not been accurately described. The scripts were returned to CBCIS along with the Department's version of the Canadian point of view for the benefit of future commentators. The CBCIS, for its part, appointed a liaison officer who commuted between its headquarters in Montreal and the Department where he was regularly briefed on its view of the world. It was clearly understood that there was to be an unbridgeable gulf between the CBCIS and the CBC National Service so that this official version of world affairs could never leap across to infect the domestic news. It seemed to work; at least there were no complaints of national news contamination and fewer from outraged allied listeners.

It was a sensible arrangement in the circumstances. In a propaganda war one either pumped out a coherent and consistent line or one kept quiet. Lying was not a part of the deal. The Department told itself (and anyone who asked) that it was merely making sure that when CBCIS spoke of Canadian government policy they got it right.

Nevertheless the system gave rise to at least one unexpected complication. It happened thus. The main CBCIS shortwave transmitter was located at Sackville, New Brunswick, a very superior location which made the CBCIS come in loud and clear deep within the Soviet Union — subject, of course, to Soviet jamming. By a quirk of geophysics, these same broadcasts could be heard equally well in Western Canada where most of our Ukrainian population is centred. This fact was not lost on one individual who was writing the Ukrainian commentaries for CBCIS, a person who also had a political point of view of his own and who became more concerned with his own agenda in Edmonton and Winnipeg than with the attempt to inform and influence the citizens of Kiev. CBCIS administration discovered that our friend was writing two scripts; one came to External, the other went on the airwaves. The one sent to the Department might, for instance, present measured criticism of some aspect of Soviet policy as viewed from Ottawa. The other, the one that was actually broadcast, was the hot gospel of Ukrainian nationalism.

The delicacy of the situation can be imagined. The CBC (International Service or not) was not only having to fire someone, but fire him, it would be said, for failing to deliver propaganda as ordered. The matter was handled with exemplary finesse by the CBCIS, whose director discovered that the individual in question had also been misusing the office stationery and its duplicating equipment in his cause. Just as Al Capone got his comeuppance for income tax evasion, our offender got his for misuse of Corporation property.

It was a recurrent complaint by missions abroad that unless they were directly involved, they received less policy guidance than the CBCIS even about our most important foreign policy initiatives. Ambassadors were left to their own devices when asked by the foreign ministry of their host government to explain what was behind the recent vote in the UN or some press report of a statement made in Ottawa. Information is the diplomat's currency and there was no effective way of getting it to most posts abroad before it was hopelessly out of date.

The people who were charged with keeping the CBCIS informed thought the same sort of material might well be sent to the Department's own posts abroad. The PITEL (Policy Information Telegram) was the result. Naturally, it would have been too expensive to have sent these "telegrams" by telegram so they went by airbag. Equally naturally, they were of little interest by the time they arrived and consequently they did not survive long in that form. Still, keeping people abroad informed continued to be a problem and a matter of constant complaint, particularly by the more remote posts which continued having to extrapolate policy even for casual inquirers. Governments at the time felt under no obligation to have a point of view on every issue as it arose and there was a certain risk involved in letting middle-grade FSOs guess, even for cocktail conversation purposes, what its policy might be on an issue the government had never looked at. Later on, in the sixties, the Department telexed CBC Radio's National News as broadcast each day. Arrangements were also made for special four-page offprints of the Toronto newspaper *The Globe and Mail*.

It has been said that the happiest nations are those that have no history — except, it might be added, for those that have no foreign policy. In the Department of External Affairs of the late forties it was possible for a young and cynical wit to claim that Canadian external policy (X) could be expressed algebraically, thus:

$$X = \frac{US + UK}{2}$$

It was almost as if Canada had no national interests that were uniquely its own, that all this country wanted was a world at peace and it would take it from there. Everything was going its way. The country had just contributed more to the winning of a just war than anyone had expected it could. Its armed forces were among the top four or five of the world, its farms and factories had served the Allied cause in ways that were still fresh in the memories of all concerned. Its diplomats had successfully eased themselves into seats at tables where none but the Great Powers had ever been seen before. More than that, they were not only being seen, they were being heard saying things that needed saying and influencing the course of events in ways that their elders and betters in the international community did not always like.

There was more. What these people were doing was not obviously self-serving. Their ideas on the framework of the United Nations were aimed at enhancing the organization, which they identified with their country's interests. Although they were occasionally patronized by those who had axes to grind, they often got their way out of sheer originality, hard work and their ability as negotiators. If the Externalites of the mid- and late forties were looked upon as do-good knights errant, their Holy Grail was the ideal of the Middle Power with Canada as the prototype.

As the Department grew to meet the challenges that were coming from the Cold War, it still held on to much of its idealistic innocence. This, combined with the air of worldliness its members had acquired in their contacts with international diplomacy, appealed strongly to its younger members in particular. However, success can be just as corrosive as power and the Department was nothing if not successful. The recognition and respect that came with its success inevitably had their effect on the Department and its members. Although great things still lay ahead, the year 1948, when its then Undersecretary, Lester Bowles Pearson, accepted a call into the political arena, it was the beginning of the end of its Golden Age of Innocence.

Middle Age
1956–1968

3

Under New Management

Just for a handful of silver he left us,
Just for a ribbon to stick in his coat.

Quoting Browning was how one FSO broke the news to his office-mates one September morning in 1948 that Mike Pearson had resigned as Undersecretary. The leading light and operating head of the Department had chosen to become a mere politician. To the casual observer, going from Undersecretary to Secretary of State for External Affairs might seem to be a logical upward movement, but in the Department, the new arrivals especially considered it to be something between desertion and a display of bad taste. The more practical-minded FSOs worried that it would be seen by the other political parties as confirmation that External was, indeed, little more than a branch of the Liberal Party, even though Mike had been careful to say in his off-hand way that he'd never thought about belonging to any particular party until he was asked to take his new job. In due course he became member of Parliament for Algoma East, assumed the leadership of the Liberal Party in January 1958 and, after a period in opposition, became Prime Minister.

Pearson's defenders argued at the time that he had done about all he could from the Undersecretary's office and if he hoped to do more to consolidate Canada in its new position in the world, it would have to be done from the political level. Nevertheless, the fact that there was a sense of betrayal testified to the strength of the feeling that the public service was one thing and politics was, and should remain, something quite separate. Ever optimistic and willing to make the most out of the inevitable, the Department soon consoled itself that one of its own was now sitting in the cabinet and that this should make life a little easier and ensure that its views were fully considered at the highest levels.

It didn't turn out to be that simple. Although there was no break in contacts and the flow of ideas and policy between the Department and cabinet was substantially unchanged, there was, for instance, no noticeable easing of the tyranny of the Treasury Board, the *bête noire* of the Department and the spoiler of so many brilliant but money-consuming ideas. Professionally, however, the Department gained by having someone in the government who knew it and knew how to use it; how to get ideas out of it and see that it did what the government wanted done with a will. The fruit of this collaboration between master and servant was a Nobel Prize for Peace.

The concept of peacekeeping which, in the form of the United Nations Emergency Force (UNEF) in the Middle East won Pearson his Nobel Prize, was not entirely new. There had been other truce supervisory organizations positioned to observe would-be warring sides and able to report which side had shot first and perhaps thereby to keep the shooting down. In Kashmir the concept had had some success, in Vietnam none at all. What was new in Pearson's UNEF proposal was the physical interposition of military forces between the contending armies so that, in effect, the UN had to be attacked before they could attack each other. The peacekeeping force had to be strong enough to defend itself, although not strong enough to impose any "solutions." The timing of the Pearson initiative in November of 1956 was as important as the idea. The British and the French were anxious to be helped out of the mess they'd made for themselves in Suez and the Americans were, ultimately, glad to see their errant allies allowed to escape. Israel was less impressed than the other interested parties since the initiative left the control of the Suez Canal in Egyptian hands.

The Pearson proposal for UNEF accomplished several things. First, it gave the UN a new instrument through which it could stop some killing and preserve the status quo until peacemaking could produce something more durable to replace it. Peacekeeping was first aid, not a cure, as the experience in Cyprus later re-emphasized. Second, it made Canada into a world authority on peacekeeping, so much so that for the next twenty years Canadian participation became the test of credibility for ventures of the kind. Third, it gave Pearson the Nobel Peace Prize for 1957, ensured him of the leadership of the Liberal Party the following year and contributed to his becoming Prime Minister of Canada in 1963. All of these events made foreign affairs a matter of serious interest to

Canadian politicians with higher ambitions — not always a positive development in terms of Canadian diplomacy, as will be seen.

The year of Suez and of UNEF, 1956, was a busy one internationally. Not until 1989 was there anything like it: a brief promise of détente between East and West on the Cold War front, followed by a deep and disturbing look into the seething internal conflicts within the Soviet Empire. Khruschev denounced Stalin (in secret) and there were uprisings in Poland and Hungary as well as the Suez emergency. Domestically, "Uncle" Louis St. Laurent was getting ready to fight his last election, which even his popular Foreign Minister, Mike Pearson, could do nothing to save from disaster. It was time for change in Canada as well, change that was to take the form of the Right Honourable John George Diefenbaker, whose ideas on foreign affairs had been shaped well before the Suez Crisis of 1956, when authorities on international affairs could still write about *The North Atlantic Triangle*, as J. B. Brebner entitled one of his books on the American–British–Canadian relationship.

Canadians of that time often talked about their country as a bridge linking Britain and the United States or even North America and Europe. The cliché was never popular in the Department. Bridges, they would say, get walked on. In any event, before the sixties were out the world's centre of gravity had moved so clearly to the western shores of the Atlantic that little more was heard of bridging that narrowing gap. The Americans had never taken the Canadian pretensions seriously, noting their own ability to communicate directly with the British — despite the common language.

Suez was the end of the era, a last gesture for the British imperial tradition. As someone said at the time, the British involvement there was like having a favourite uncle charged with rape. Canada's part in the aftermath, the creation of the United Nations Emergency Force, was at least partly intended to help the British and French. Nevertheless, it did nothing for bilateral relationships with those countries. Probably for the first time it put Canada on the same side as the United States and against Britain. After Suez, British influence on and interest in Canada very gradually lessened until all that was left of this very special relationship were some bureaucratic procedures, constitutional similarities and perhaps some cultural biases.

This was the situation in June of 1957 when the country treated itself to a new government headed by an individual who, over the years in opposition, had sent unmixed signals to the people of the

Department. For reasons that are hard to explain in the light of the information we've been given by Basil Robinson's *Diefenbaker's World*, the new Prime Minister was believed to have little interest in foreign affairs, although he did seem to enjoy giving External the rough side of a pretty abrasive tongue. Robinson's book shows that Diefenbaker's real feelings were complicated and that, in his own way, he took a great interest foreign affairs and may actually have had some respect for the Department.

John Diefenbaker's constant jibes about External Affairs, about the "Pearsonalities" being a limb of the Liberal Party of Canada, were understandable, but Diefenbaker was given to oversimplification. No man is a hero to his valet and Mike Pearson was no exception. Liked he certainly was in the Department; it would have been hard for him not to be. He was admired too, but less universally. Some felt he had abandoned the Department, and others foresaw how his decision to go into politics as a Liberal would affect the opposition parties' attitudes toward the Department. But the Diefenbaker charge of partisanship (to the extent it was true) was anything but deliberate; it was not even conscious. Those who ran the Department, notably Norman Robertson himself, were writing and speaking generally about the virtues of a professional public service and the necessity of public servants remaining anonymous and apolitical long before Diefenbaker appeared on the scene. This was certainly the doctrine preached by the University of the East Block.

Nevertheless, there were the long-standing links with Liberal governments. Apart from Pearson there was the unique relationship between Mackenzie King and Norman Robertson who has been described as an unelected member of his cabinet. Moreover, collaboration between members of External and their political masters sometimes developed into strong personal friendships, although there is little evidence that this amounted to political support. The rule was that personal friendship should not imply political sympathy. Your loyalty was to the government of the day or you resigned.

Within the privacy of their own offices the people in the Department were usually more critical of the government than they were of the Opposition because the government had access to better information than their opponents — not to mention the Department's superior advice. FSOs with avowed political inclinations were rare and rarer still were those, if any, who actually worked for or even kept in touch with politicians for partisan purposes. When the rules were changed in the late sixties and seventies to allow public servants to run for office without first resigning, the reform was by no means applauded in External. A few took advantage of the new rules but the great majority of the colleagues saw themselves as full-time public servants with no inclination to get into politics, directly or otherwise. All this having been said, in the election of 1957 even partisan Tories in the Department might have found it difficult to vote against Mike Pearson's cool and analytical view of Canada's place in the world and for John G. Diefenbaker's "northern vision."

In practice, in spite of his verbal scorn, Diefenbaker interfered less with the professional operation of the Department than some of his successors. But the mistrust was there and in the Diefenbaker years the Department got its first taste of having its views ignored, its people by-passed and its advice unsought. It would get more of the same later.

Foreign affairs are about politics, and the similarities between domestic and external politics are greater than the differences. The single most important difference, however, is that domestic policies can be legislated into action while foreign policies must be negotiated. If a government has the popular support and can raise the money, it can do just about what it likes on its own territory. In the foreign environment, unless it intends to go to war, it must get the approval of the other countries concerned. This distinction has not always been understood by politicians who arrive on the scene with a majority in Parliament and declare their intention, in effect, to legislate a new foreign policy. They naturally do not take kindly to being told it won't work that way.

When the Conservative government took office, the Department was trying to tell its new political masters what they needed to know, while the new government was trying to get its message through to the Department. Members of new governments want to be seen doing conspicuous things in prominent places and very few are contented to direct proceedings from the background. Moreover, combined with a natural reluctance to take advice from underlings, there is an unwillingness among politicians generally to believe that diplomats are any better at wheeling and dealing than they are themselves. Diefenbaker's early promise to swing a large part of Canada's external trade toward the United Kingdom was a fine illustration of all the errors a new government is likely to make. Without waiting for advice, he declared a policy that was beyond his government's power to implement. He had to live with the consequences.

After the death of the first Progressive Conservative External Affairs Minister, Sidney Smith, in 1959, a scant year and a half after taking office, and the eventual appointment of Howard Green, things settled down in the Department. Green came to External from, of all places, Public Works, then best known as the government's patronage pork barrel. Little was expected of him but Green turned out to be a pleasant surprise. He brought with him two great assets. He was trusted by the Prime Minister, which meant that proposals from him would probably be listened to; and he liked people — even, it turned out, the people in External. And they returned the compliment. Although those on the firing line with the PM, like Basil Robinson, led very difficult lives indeed, the rest found shelter behind the deceptively frail form of Howard Green.

From June of 1957 until Pearson formed his first minority government in April of 1963, the government's main concern in the international field had to do with Canada-US relations. Diefenbaker seemed neither to like nor trust the American government of the day and John Kennedy reciprocated the feelings fully. Yet it was during the Diefenbaker administration that some of the most far-reaching decisions were made about the bilateral relationship. It is ironic that Diefenbaker's attempts to redirect Canadian business activity toward Britain and the Commonwealth (and presumably away from the United States) came to nothing while, despite some foot dragging, he committed Canada to greater Canadian involvement in continental defences under American leadership.

The North American Air Defence (Norad) agreement was, in effect, found in the Pearson government's basket of unfinished business where it was, no doubt, "maturing." In spite of its dark view of American machinations, the Diefenbaker government quickly put the agreement into effect, perhaps for no better reason than that this new government also wanted to be seen making decisions. After all, the terms had all been negotiated under Mike Pearson himself, who would therefore be in no position to attack the agreement from the Opposition benches.

Would a government headed by Pearson have signed the Norad accord in the end? It was Pearson who was said to have commented that if you were a beautiful woman (Canada), it was better to be in bed with fourteen men (as in Nato) than with one (as in Norad).

The agreement that was negotiated was no doubt the best obtainable, but there was still a preference within the Department for having the defence of North America tied in with Nato. The Americans were not at all happy about the idea of letting the Europeans stick their noses into matters so vital to American security, but that need not have been the end of the matter. There was room for some middle ground. The fact that the draft was lying about until after the election suggests that the Liberal government might have had some reservations about it.

The Diefenbaker government's greatest international challenge came in October 1962 when the US government discovered a build-up in Cuba of Soviet missiles that were capable of striking deep into the continental United States. In a series of exchanges with the Soviet government, Kennedy forced Khruschev to choose, in effect, between withdrawing them or facing a war with the United States. The Soviet missiles were withdrawn and soon after Khruschev was forced from office for his "adventurism."

Throughout the crisis, the Nato allies were kept informed and their co-operation was sought in bringing their national forces to a high state of alert partly in case war did result but also, no doubt, to convince Soviet intelligence listening in on Nato defence networks that the West was united and meant business. Diefenbaker's reluctance to act swiftly or automatically on a matter of such importance was awkward but, in the light of Canadian history, it was also understandable. Although the government had been kept informed to a degree, it had had no part in any of the decisions that had led up to the delivery of Kennedy's ultimatum. Canada had gone into World War II without having taken part in the process that led up to it, but the assumption in Ottawa was that things had changed since 1939 and that if there was to be another war, we would have more to say about it. Moreover, Diefenbaker's reluctance to follow the American lead had begun some time before October 1962. His government had resisted American urgings to break relations with the Cuban government after Castro, having taken power in 1959, later announced Cuba's alignment with the Soviet Union.

Although Diefenbaker was a voluble anti-communist he was obviously not a hawk. His government had acquired Bomarc missiles, then hesitated in providing the nuclear warheads that made them effective. This inaction would certainly have been regarded by the American government as affecting their national security, a very serious matter indeed. It also had some dire consequences for Mr Diefenbaker's government.

Howard Green, then Secretary of State for External Affairs, played a significant part in the non-decision on the Bomarc, which eventually led to a revolt within the government. The government lost a vote of confidence; for the first time a Canadian government fell on a matter of external policy.

The Department itself was divided on the notion of Canada's defence commitment. There were those who simply accepted our Nato and Norad commitments at their face value, and those who tried to distinguish (particularly in regard to Norad) between the cost of defending North America, for which Canada had a responsibility, and the cost of defending the United States' superpower status, which was primarily an American affair. Nato was where we sought to exercise our influence on policy decisions. Norad was seen as a purely military arrangement, not a policy-making institution through which American policy could be influenced. Because we lived in the neighbourhood of a superpower, we had to provide the facilities it needed to defend its status, but we should not have to share in the expenses as well. As some members of the Department would note, the Americans had to defend Canada in order to defend themselves. But they all knew that if we failed to do what had to be done, the Americans would insist on doing it themselves.

External's view of the US relationship precluded anything that resembled direct defiance of American wishes that were based on the matter of security. The usual approach was to concede what could not be denied but leave a way open for either reconsidering or diluting those parts of the arrangement that were not thought to be in Canada's own interests. When Pearson came to power in 1963, nuclear warheads for Bomarcs were accepted, but eventually the Bomarc missiles were phased out and so was the storage of nuclear warheads in Canada.

There were many in the Department who were willing to write off the Diefenbaker years as a time of bumbling indecision, an unfortunate interruption in the otherwise steady march of Canada from obscurity to the dignity of Middle Power status and on into United Nations prominence. But with the advantage of hindsight that would be an unfair judgement. Diefenbaker, perhaps more than any new prime minister up to then, actually tried to give Canadian foreign policy not just his own imprint but a new spin. He was more of a nationalist than an internationalist and he continued to see

Britain as a counterweight in dealing with the United States. Unfortunately for him, Canadian national feeling was weak and the British had their own interests to consider in their dealings with the Americans.

Diefenbaker always believed that his downfall had been engineered in Washington. He had a case, although he may have overstated it. In the end he was rejected by the Canadian electorate which includes large numbers of Canadians who, without being disloyal, consider that no one in Canada can really know what is going on in the world. In the past, these people have looked to Britain as the source of wisdom and felt most comfortable when following a lead that came from London. The same sort of deference came to be applied to the United States. Some of this feeling could be a natural consequence of the flood of information that comes from that quarter. In any event, when an American president disapproved of a Canadian prime minister as Kennedy was known to have disapproved of Diefenbaker, there were voters who would have been influenced.

During his time in office, Diefenbaker obviously attached sufficient importance to the American relationship to be wary of it. He foresaw and tried to deflect the movement toward greater continental integration. Where others, Pearson before him and Trudeau later, had this same objective in mind and tried to slow down the process, Diefenbaker actually tried to reverse it and restore the old three-way Atlantic balancing relationship. It was not an attainable objective. Diefenbaker's failure showed that it would take more than a pious declaration of intent to keep Canada out of a closer continental relationship.

4

Special Relationships

A country's foreign policy consists of the goals that it sets for itself in the international environment. Its diplomacy is the means by which it tries to reach them. As John Diefenbaker learned, neither foreign policy nor diplomacy can be changed by whim. By definition, a country's international interests lie outside its own control. The courses open to it are also limited by objective facts beyond its reach: the location of the country, the history of its relations with its neighbours, the sort of neighbours it has, its natural endowments, how it earns its living, its own traditions and internal cohesion. None of these things change from day to day, and the policies as well as the diplomacy that evolve to deal with them are not subject to casual change either. Priorities may be juggled and styles can vary but only occasionally do circumstances arise when governments are presented with opportunities to strike off in new directions. It takes more than a mere act of political will to produce a new foreign policy.

In the 1950s some of the assumptions on which Canadian diplomacy had been based underwent a fundamental change. The nature and extent of British influence on Canadian diplomacy, if not on its foreign policy, have already been noted. The relative importance of Britain on the international scene underwent a serious reassessment with the end of the war and this, as well as the wartime collaboration between Roosevelt and Churchill, affected the way both the British and the Americans saw their relations developing. France, always the object of special attention for any Canadian government, was fully occupied with its own internal and colonial problems in the early postwar years.

Consequently, Canada began to look less to Europe for its ideas about peace and war and began looking increasingly to the south. The situation envisaged by Escott Reid in 1943, of moving from a quasi-colonial relationship with London to a comparable relationship with Washington, was already being realized a mere fifteen years after he had warned against it.

Well into the sixties, long after Ottawa was looking more often to Washington than to London, members of the Department found that relations with the British foreign service at any diplomatic post were still the easiest. This was partly because some remnant of the umbilical cord between Canada and Britain remained, partly because the Commonwealth provided reasons for contact over and above bilateral affairs, and partly because the Department had been modelled on British practice and it spoke a very similar bureaucratic language.

Until some time after 1950, for instance, formal despatches from heads of post to the Secretary of State for External Affairs began, "Sir, I have the honour to ..." and ended with, "I have the honour to be, Sir, your obedient servant, XYZ." The obligatory opening was a challenge and a discipline. It forced the writer to say what the communication was about within the span of a sentence and thereby helped him focus his thoughts. The less formal "letter" began, "Dear Department" or "Dear European [Division]" or even "Dear So-and-so" [the occupant of the office concerned] and was signed off, "Yours ever, [signature] Chancery." All of these forms had been taken straight out of Foreign Office procedure. By the sixties they would be replaced by the more impersonal Despatch and Numbered Letter forms. There were legal as well as cosmetic reasons behind the change. The lawyers discovered well after the war that any document addressed to an individual by name could be regarded as the property of that person, which could have serious consequences for the Departmental archives.

During this same period, except for the Canadian coat of arms, the red morocco despatch boxes in which official documents were carried around in the Department and on delegations abroad were direct copies of the British models, with the carrying handle on the same side as the hinge so papers would fall out if you tried to carry one off without locking it. In security and intelligence operations not only were the methods British, so were many of the people who ran them. The rest had had British training. For many years the Department shared some activities with the British, particularly in matters of security.

There was an enormous advantage in having a freely available model to copy during the Department's years of expansion, and the British were always glad to help. If External had been obliged to create a diplomatic apparatus from scratch, it would not have been able to perform the prodigies of work it did in the early postwar years.

British motives in helping the new Canadian Foreign Service as generously as they did would have included a desire to influence the end product. Information that was received from the British in great quantities and on all sorts of subjects obviously had to be read with the source in mind, like any other information. The most the British could have hoped was that, other things being equal, where no direct Canadian interest was concerned, Canada would tilt in their direction. At times there would have been a tendency in the Department to follow British leads as a sort of fail-safe reaction, but as Canada came to have more posts of its own abroad and got more information from these and other sources, the occasions on which there was no specifically Canadian position became rarer.

Even at the height of British influence on the Department, however, not all British diplomatic practices became standard operating procedure. Canadians, for instance, never became as good at managing their contacts in foreign countries as the British were. It somehow went against the Canadian grain to cultivate people for the purpose of exploiting them, although that was the ultimate justification for the foreign service representation allowance. It is not being cynical to observe that the British excel at establishing a personal relationship with the people who count. Over the years every British diplomatic mission has built up lists of local friends which are handed on from one diplomatic incumbent to the next.

The idea of "the ruling few" is the very British working assumption that in every country there are a small number of people who really run things and they are not always the obvious ones. Great attention is given to identifying these eminences, grey or otherwise, and then cultivating a personal relationship with them. Influencing people is the essence of diplomatic negotiation and the British are better at it than most.

Many other British models never caught on. Black homburgs did appear in Ottawa, but bowlers were rare and no one wore the "short black," the chancery jacket with grey striped trousers (not pants), unless they were attending a presentation of credentials at Government House that day.

Abroad, while the war was still a very recent memory, the emotional mix of friendship and patronage that had characterized Canadian involvement in British operations during the war continued to apply between Canadian and British missions on foreign posts. Commonwealth heads of mission met quite frequently in most capitals to talk about "the locals," or more politely, to exchange views on current issues. Canadians gained a lot in these exchanges, the British having sources of information others could only dream about. Nevertheless, as time went on it became obvious that our interests differed and occasionally conflicted. With or without Suez, by the end of the fifties it was clearly time to get out from under the mother hen and go pecking about for one's self.

The process of distancing Canadian diplomacy from that of Britain had begun while the war was still on and it was consciously pursued by people who had themselves strong British ties, especially a British education. (According to R. Barry Farrell in *The Making of Canadian Foreign Policy,* in 1950, 27 percent of all FSOs had gone to a British university. In the upper echelons, the proportion would have been higher.) In action at an international conference, some could easily have given the impression of actually being British, which would have added to the Department's defensiveness and contributed to the changes that were to come about.

There were times when the British government of the day (when Edward Heath was Prime Minister, for instance) regarded the Commonwealth as a millstone to be offloaded as quickly as was decently possible. But in diplomacy, even declining assets are not liquidated merely for the sake of tidiness. For Canada, the Commonwealth had a particular use. As the United States was not a member, Canada was the principal source of North American input. Moreover, the Commonwealth was a potential source, if not of support, at least of sympathy and influence for Canada in the Third World. Canada was sometimes seen as the main pillar of the Commonwealth, which occasionally became a minor irritation to British governments.

In any event, by the mid-sixties, neither Britain nor the Commonwealth could be seen as much of a counterweight in dealings with the United States. Bilateral relations with Britain remained good, even close, but no Canadian government could expect Britain to adjust its own highly prized relationship with the United States on Canada's account. Above all, common membership in Nato had superseded the North Atlantic triangle.

In the adjustments that followed Suez, British diplomacy moved quickly to repair the London–Washington axis and move Britain from being an international force in its own right to becoming an influential friend of the American superpower. The diminished geopolitical position of Britain was accepted as a new point of departure and the impressive diplomatic apparatus that had been built up to serve the dominant superpower of its time was consolidated, even cut back, but it was not abandoned. Nor did Britain change its world power terms of reference: to keep in touch with and influence events wherever they could affect British interests directly or indirectly. The adjustment to the new status had begun with the wartime Churchill–Roosevelt association. Successive governments gave further signs of believing that Britain's interests could best be served by influencing the United States. This became a fixed element in the British world outlook through all sorts of British governments, but it flourished most under the Thatcher regime during the Reagan years. Apart from a slight glitch over Grenada in October of 1983, mutual support was the rule.

How much the British, or any foreign government, can actually influence American decisions is an open question. It is, however, probably true to say that if any foreigners are able to influence the United States in a matter of first importance, the British have the best chance — far better, for instance, than the Canadian government, whose influence rarely extends beyond matters of bilateral concern.

The British probably have deep background information on more parts of the world than any other government. British diplomats are perhaps the best trained in the collection, collation and distribution of information, and their competence in this area has remained convincing in spite of some horrendous pratfalls, like the Burgess, Maclean, Philby, Blake and Lonsdale affairs.

Before the end of the sixties, there was nothing left of the North Atlantic triangle and although Nato was firmly in place, the three sides of the triangle had become three bilateral axes: London–Washington; Ottawa–Washington; and a much-diminished Ottawa–London axis. Canada was on its own in dealing with the United States as it had never been before. At the same time, the issues involved were closer to Canada's vital interests than they had been with Britain for many years.

Dealing with Americans on the personal level was almost always an easy and relaxed process for the Department, although dealing with American institutions is often extremely frustrating. It is not the American personality but the American constitution that shapes the way the United States conducts its foreign relations. No other major world power operates under so many apparently inhibiting rules. Fortunately for American diplomacy, ways have been found of coping with some of these restrictions without either ignoring them or applying them. If they so choose, Americans have shown they can even wage war without following the constitutional provisions for doing so. Depending on internal circumstances, the constitution can make it easier or more difficult for US diplomats to deal with other countries.

The right of the US Senate to press its advice and withhold its consent in international affairs begins with the appointment of its foreign secretary — the Secretary of State — and its Ambassadors. It extends to the declaration of war and the ratification of formal international agreements. On the face of it, the veto over appointments alone could bring American diplomacy to a standstill were it not for a faithful core of career people and an understanding that the president should normally be allowed to appoint whomever he pleases to these positions.

In the matter of making treaties, the Senate can be circumvented, as it was when the Norad Agreement with Canada was concluded. This treaty-in-all-but-name and its many renewals have always taken the form of an exchange of notes in which each country expresses its intention to do some specified things in concert with the other party. It is not binding in law within the United States, but it works where both parties want it to. On other occasions, such as the free trade negotiation, the Senate can put limits on the exercise of its own powers; thus, the so-called fast-track process, by which the Senators agreed to accept or reject a proposition within a reasonable period of time and without amendment.

On other occasions, and particularly when a threat to American security can be claimed, a bipartisan approach may be negotiated within Congress giving the administration greater latitude than a strict interpretation of the constitution would permit. This was the process by which the Senate gave President Johnson the power to wage war in Vietnam virtually without limitations. It was passed in the Senate after the Gulf of Tonkin incident, and no doubt contributed to the war's messy conclusion as the consensus fell apart.

Despite appearances to the contrary, the constitutional limitations on the administration can actually be a help in dealing with other countries. The requirement that the Senate ratify international agreements has become a part of the US bargaining process that leaves the other side guessing what the ultimate American position is going to be. Negotiators for the other side know that, after satisfying those who are acting in the name of the United States, they still may see the Senate reject the result of the negotiation or attach new conditions to whatever is submitted to it. American negotiators can, of course, use this to good effect.

Negotiators for most other countries carry "full powers" to a negotiating table and if their governments fail to ratify what their plenipotentiary has approved (presumably on instructions from home) it would amount to a defeat of the government or evidence of bad faith. When Woodrow Wilson failed to have the provisions for the creation of the League of Nations ratified by the Senate, it was a personal embarrassment, nothing more. Although sovereign states cannot legally be bound in advance and plenipotentiaries can always be repudiated, negotiating with the United States does present special problems.

Canada has found itself left at the altar on several occasions during the past hundred years and more. The most recent example was the ill-fated Georges Bank agreement of the late seventies, which both delegations had approved on the basis of instructions from home. Canada ratified but the United States did not. In the free trade instance, the "fast-track" arrangements laid down by the US Senate provided for it to be kept posted on the progress of the negotiations and to make its input as the negotiations proceeded. This process went some way toward guaranteeing that what was negotiated would be ratified. It obviated the game of blind man's bluff that applies when no one, including the American negotiators, knows what the Senate's final position is going to be.

There is another difficulty in dealing diplomatically with the United States. Every eight years at most, and often after only four, the top people who have conducted its foreign affairs up to then are changed. Every Ambassador and most of the upper echelons of the State Department must tender their resignations when a president leaves office. The new president may then appoint new people whose main claim to office is that they helped him get elected. At best those appointed positions well below the policy-making level are given to individuals who have had either scant contact with international affairs or a largely academic knowledge of them. Every country, including Canada, has had the experience of having the United States represented in their capital by someone who had no qualifications for the job.

The United States has a very good career foreign service, far better than anyone would expect considering that the best jobs are normally out of its members' reach. At every American embassy of any consequence there is a deputy chief of mission (DCM), a career person who keeps the show on the road, sometimes including control of the damage done by an unfortunate Ambassador. This is not to say there is no place in diplomacy for political appointees, but the American way of selecting them and coping with them has not always served the best interests of either the United States or the international community.

American diplomats are sometimes criticized for justifying action by reference to some moral principle rather than "national interest," which is the more commonly accepted basis for international action. In the matter of recognizing governments, the Canadian view has been that the formality is largely a legal-technical matter. Is the government in effective control over the territory it claims? Is it likely to last for a while? Will it at least try to keep its international commitments? If the answers are all "yes," and we wish to do business with that country, we should recognize the government in question. The United States, on the other hand, linked recognition with approval and refused to extend recognition to Communist China and Castro's Cuba on what can best be called "moral grounds." No one can say what would have been the effect had the Americans done otherwise, but common sense suggests that cutting off communication with opponents is not the most obvious way of trying to influence them.

Most great powers have a sense of mission, a destiny or some philosophical base, that can convert what would be simply a selfish act in an individual into a service to a Higher Cause. Even so, few modern states involve the Deity in their day-to-day affairs as much as the United States. One Canadian Ambassador in Washington, a reasonably devout Christian, eventually declined to take part in that peculiarly Washingtonian event, the Prayer Breakfast, on the ground that it seemed to be making political mileage out of God. A more cynical person might have gone just to be seen. Americans can and do link their national interests to a Higher Cause. It may or may not bring the Almighty on side but it undoubtedly helps ensure popular support for their foreign policy initiatives.

Whatever effect the *Gott mit Uns* phenomenon may have internally, it is going too far to expect others to accept that same evaluation of one's own motives. The "White Man's Burden" no doubt helped the individual Englishman justify his preferred position but it is doubtful if it impressed the African whose burden was more tangible. The Soviet Union might have fooled some of its own by telling the Hungarians in 1956 that the Red Army that was suppressing them was merely a servant of History and the Working Class. Neither the Deity nor History is very often invoked during international negotiations; the normal difficulties of cross-cultural communication are severe enough. But it is wise to remember in dealing with diplomats from countries that have identifiable ideologies, officially recognized or not, that their basic beliefs about themselves may well be relevant to the negotiation.

The American use of the word "doctrine" for "foreign policy" smacks of both moral authority and a profound level of thought approaching a philosophic truth. It also confers an aura of immutability that is uncomfortable in a diplomatic context. Take, for instance, the Monroe Doctrine, which was enunciated early in the last century to warn European powers not already present in the Americas to stay away. This unilateral American declaration is sometimes referred to as if it were a principle of international law. To the countries that are affected by it, the Monroe Doctrine has been a shield against oppression by erstwhile imperial powers wanting to reclaim liberated colonies. It has also been a warning to countries in the Americas that they should be careful in choosing their friends. Other powerful countries have adopted, or have tried to adopt, similar policies in respect of their spheres of influence — the so-called Brezhnev Doctrine proclaiming the irreversibility of "socialism," for instance.

The most potent words in the American diplomatic vocabulary are "national security." This has been an imperative imposed on every American government since George Washington to keep the country impregnable against any conceivable enemy. There is now no such enemy anywhere on the horizon, but the principle remains and is being applied to the preservation of America's position in the world. There should be no doubt that if the American people can be persuaded that their country's "national security" is at stake, they will pay whatever price is asked of them to ensure it.

The United States has shown itself capable of great acts of generosity, as befits its place in the world and the open-handedness of its people. This makes it all the more difficult to accept some of the actions that have been taken by some US governments in their Latin American and Caribbean "backyard." The ability to be one thing at home and another abroad is, perhaps, a function of greatness and has been shared in one form or another by all countries that achieve Great Power status. *Raison d'état*, the right to be a judge in one's own cause, goes with being a Great Power and there is no point in reacting with shock to actions based on it. There is a point in being prepared for the United States to act to preserve its position. If anyone doubts the ability of the United States to act to protect its interests without regard for the rules, they need look no farther than Central America from Guatemala to Panama.

This list of the special features of American diplomacy is by no means complete. Most of the things mentioned are either sources of the strength that has made the United States the dominant power it is, or they are the consequences of having become the dominant power. Canadians may admire or dislike the things that made or keep America great but if we wish to live peaceably and independently alongside it we need to know how it sees itself and learn how to deal with, or live with, what we know. It is said that Canadians think they know all they need to about their great neighbour. Somewhere within the collective mind this may be true. Nevertheless, at the individual and personal levels, Canadians have been known to discount or ignore aspects of the relationship that are inconvenient and write off as chronic anti-Americans those who keep reminding them of the less familiar side. Therefore, although difficult, it is important that Canadian diplomats be able to look at even the nicest people with fishy eyes — cool and unblinking.

The United States is, of course, the great constant in Canadian foreign policy and has been since well before the Department came into existence. And Canada has been a matter of interest to the United States since a revolutionary Congress invited Quebec (in French) to join in their struggle against the imperial power. In spite of occasional references to "manifest destiny" and the "ripe pear" on the one side and "no truck nor trade with the Yankees" on the other, the relations between the two countries have been exemplary. This has not been accidental. All recent American governments have bent over backwards to avoid even the appearance of bullying. Witness the American acceptance of the understanding which, until the free trade deal of 1989 put just about everything on the same table, ensured that outstanding bilateral issues would be dealt with separately and on their own merits. Canada, for its part, has done its utmost to make sure that the United States got from Canada everything it could legitimately claim as essential to its national security.

As the most powerful country on earth, the United States inevitably inspires admiration and affection as well as envy and fear. It has shown itself capable of far-seeing acts of generosity, and most

Americans would include in this the enormous burden its taxpayers carry for the defence of the "free world," including Canada. They are therefore very sensitive to what they regard as anti-Americanism. American diplomats in Canada have been known to express the view that those who claim not to be anti-American, only pro-Canadian, are merely justifying their anti-Americanism. The sensible desire of most Canadians not to appear anti-American has inhibited public discussion of some of the difficulties in dealing with their neighbours.

A reluctance to talk about the United States as one might about any other country would bode ill for the future relationship. As close neighbours the inhabitants of both countries know each other's shortcomings even when they seem not to know their own. Both have different sets of interests and serious, if different, internal problems. There is a risk, particularly if the two countries approach economic unity, that Canadians could be expected to ignore these differences and identify with the goals and aspirations of the major partner, particularly in the foreign field. At the same time the cultural flood that comes north across the frontier obscures and will eventually eliminate differences in outlook and perceptions of interests unless they are countered by other opinions and attitudes. Canadian efforts to preserve Canada's differences will not be effective if they must always be accompanied by an apology for doing so.

Assumption into the United States may indeed be Canada's manifest destiny. It may well be a ripe pear about to fall into Columbia's lap but here is no question of a modern government of the United States attempting to shake the tree. The American people wouldn't stand for it on moral grounds. If Canadians lose their independence, it will be because they themselves have willed it. No amount of diplomacy can save those who have lost their desire to be different.

Preserving differences (and perhaps creating new ones) has been the hallmark of French diplomacy. Although next to Britain and the United States, France has been the greatest external influence on Canada, the Department never saw the French foreign service as a role model and no doubt was the poorer for it. Nevertheless, and partly because of its own inadequate representation of French-speaking Canada during the fifties and early sixties, it treated French colleagues with the greatest respect.

Some French diplomats were brilliant and charming, others brilliant and abrasive, but all were conscious of their membership in a profession that their country perfected two centuries ago (many would say) in the person of the great Charles-Maurice de Talleyrand. French diplomats are probably the best equipped of any in terms of knowledge and training to do the job expected of them. The French educational system might well have been designed to turn out public servants. The best of its products are further honed and polished by the government's own École nationale d'administration from which it gets most of its diplomats.

Diplomats serving France are, perhaps still, the envy of their trade. It may seem different to those who are closer to the French political scene, but to the outsider French voters are essentially inward looking; as long as their government does nothing to disturb their normally agreeable lives, they really don't care what foreign policy their government pursues. Thus the French foreign ministry, the Quai d'Orsay, would resemble the position External Affairs occupied during the early postwar years when foreign affairs was a matter of interest to a only select and sympathetic few. This provides a wonderful base from which to conduct diplomacy, especially when dealing with less fortunate foreign ministries that are constantly having to defend their actions before their own public. The downside, of course, is that freedom from criticism can encourage self-deception and an unhealthy detachment from the realities of national interest — as seen in the Canadian context.

In the French context, nothing of the sort happens. It may be an oversimplification to say that French diplomats know without having to wait for instructions what their government's policy on virtually any issue is likely to be. Yet the immediate interests of France, coolly rationalized and buttressed with weighty arguments, can be worked out by Ambassadors at their posts without need for instructions from home unless or until persuasive reasons appear for changing direction. Things like radioactive fall-out in the Pacific or the proliferation of nuclear technology or the sale of Mirage aircraft to both sides in the Middle East did not create the same problems for French governments that they would in other countries.

The ability of French diplomats to get the best of all worlds is legendary. They can argue persuasively why France, sometimes alone, cannot support a position taken by its friends and allies. Under General de Gaulle, French diplomacy was able to take France out of joint military planning in Nato without jeopardizing the protection the alliance gave the country. Geography has made France indispensable both to the defence of Western Europe and in the building of the European Community. Negotiations within the EC and Nato are replete with instances of French obduracy, unshakable in its confidence of France's indispensability.

Although French attitudes are often resented, France's actions are entirely in accord with the standards that apply in international affairs. Most other governments would like to follow France's example but few of them have either the commanding geopolitical position or the popular support that French governments can usually command in matters of foreign affairs. French diplomats are well aware of this reputation and can argue with great conviction that what looks to others like a purely self-serving posture also happens to be in the best interests of humanity. They can understand others who see all this as excessively selfish national behaviour, but they can defend that too. They can say in truth that in a world of sovereign states, devoid of anything that resembles an international legal system, every government is morally obliged to look to its own nation's interests, first, last and all the time. Anything else is either quixotic nonsense or simple hypocrisy.

Beginning at least with Talleyrand (1754–1838), France's diplomats have been particularly skilful in being on all sides of important issues. Although France under Napoleon Bonaparte brought ideas of liberty and nationalism to much of Europe, it made few friends among its neighbours. When the war was over, Talleyrand, who had served every government of France from the late stages of the Revolution, through most of the Napoleonic era to the restoration of the monarchy and beyond, was able to present his country as the prime victim of Napoleon's adventures. In 1815 Talleyrand left the Congress of Vienna almost as though his country had been on the winning side. In the process, he had contributed heavily to the new European order, which turned out to be a wise and generous settlement that spared Europe from another such war for almost a hundred years.

Beginning even before General de Gaulle's 1967 *"Vive le Québec libre"* speech, and for a decade or more afterward, poor old External found itself up against the spiritual children of Talleyrand. The Department and particularly its members who were in the front line, notably Jules Léger as Ambassador in Paris, conducted themselves in the only way they could have, with heroic patience grounded in the knowledge that de Gaulle was mortal and he had no comparable successor.

Canada could not write off or ignore France as, for instance, American governments occasionally tried to do, partly because an important part of Canada needed the cultural comfort that only France could provide. But it was also partly because France would not be ignored. De Gaulle saw Canada (or at least Quebec) as an instrument for French policy in North America. In his conception of France as a world power, there would be an important role for a French nation strategically situated on the flank of the United States.

France, perhaps more than other countries with highly developed cultures, carried its heritage into its foreign policy. *La mission civilisatrice* was not just to preserve and advance the language of Molière and to share French cultural wealth with the world; it also served to advance France's policies of the day. Canada was an obvious case in point.

The Canadian diplomats who dealt with France during the troublesome sixties were mainly from French-speaking areas but, apart from fluency in the language, they were no better prepared than their anglophone counterparts to deal with the powerful, single-minded, subtle and occasionally ruthless Quai d'Orsay which, at the time, was intent on playing a part in Canadian politics. Moreover, France's motives were not always easy to fathom. There was nothing Canada could give France that it could not have obtained by more conventional methods.

The most obvious explanation of de Gaulle's interest in the Quebec politics would seem to be that, once removed from its Canadian context, Quebec could be made to serve as a French thorn in the side of the United States. Quebec, situated on the northeastern approaches to the North American continent, would be a matter of concern to the United States in much the same way that France's own geographical position was a matter of concern to Europe. However, it is difficult to imagine how de Gaulle could think the United States could be bargained with in this way, even supposing de Gaulle could have persuaded Quebec to sacrifice its own interests to those of a resurgent France.

No one knows for sure if this was, in fact, the way de Gaulle thought about Quebec, but there were some strange ideas about Quebec and Canada operating within the French foreign service. During this period, it was not unknown for a French diplomat to inform third parties, and in the presence of a Canadian colleague, that French language and culture in Canada had been destroyed by the English-speaking majority as a matter of policy. Canadians of

French origin in France would be told much the same sort of thing and be expected to accept the proposition that their culture had, in fact, been lost. This is not to say that French diplomats concerned with Canadian affairs were ignorant of the true state of affairs in Quebec. Rather, it illustrates a state of mind among French official-dom which, in this context, did not serve French interests in Quebec very effectively.

As the virtual prototype, if not the inventor of the modern nation-state, France has never fully accepted Canada's claim to nationhood. Canadians were too regionally minded and scattered and too cultur-ally divided to qualify under the nineteenth-century rules. It would be natural for France to be disturbed by the possibility of Canada, and with it Quebec, being drawn into the more conventional nation-state to the south and by the threat that this would present to what was left of French civilization in North America. This alone could be reason enough for taking a hand in Canadian politics.

The significance of General de Gaulle's famous *"Vive le Québec libre"* spoken from a balcony in Montreal in 1967 was debated in the Department as it was throughout the country. Mr. Pearson de-clared the general's utterance to be unacceptable, and de Gaulle promptly left the country without completing his visit. Although there were some dissenting voices, particularly to the effect that the government had overreacted, there was general agreement that the General's statement was not a slip of the tongue. After General de Gaulle's visitation, the government could no longer assume that the influence of France would always be benign so far as Canada was concerned. Now one thing had become clear: Canada's relations with France had become a matter of prime concern not just within the Department, but at all its diplomatic posts.

It is clear that Canada had access to a pretty sophisticated network dedicated to the reading of diplomatic communications. (See *Spy Wars* by J.L. Granatstein and David Stafford.) In spite of the myth about allies not spying on allies, it would have been a strange lapse, in the circumstances, if no effort had been made during those years of tension to find out just what was going on within France's diplo-matic and consular missions in Canada. Undoubtedly, according to *Spy Wars,* the Communications Security Establishment had the means. Unless someone can suggest a reason why French ciphers might not have been attacked, it would be reasonable to assume that at least some of them were actually read and that Canadian responses at the time would have taken the information obtained into account.

French diplomats were not by any means all Gaullists and those who were not were frequently apologetic for their more zealous colleagues. Diplomats from other countries would tell Canadian colleagues, privately of course, how impossible de Gaulle's France was to deal with and generally make sympathetic noises. Nevertheless, the divisions within Canada which the de Gaulle affair had highlighted did adversely affect other diplomatic assessments of Canada, and specifically its ability to play an active international role while coping with a difficult internal situation.

Diplomats of all countries often wonder how much influence they have. Not how much they should have, but how seriously their carefully crafted advice is taken by their own governments. All are conscious of belonging to a great international communications system that gives the planet whatever coherence it has.

No diplomat could work on a post abroad in any capacity for a day without realizing that this work was a part of a bigger picture beginning with the representatives of the host government who had to be dealt with on a day-to-day basis and then with the representatives of other countries on the post with whom tradition and self-interest required that contact be maintained. It was to be expected that among the pros there would be a camaraderie, almost a trade union spirit, that went beyond the preoccupations of one's own country. It is not a question of conflicting loyalties and it doesn't hamper work on behalf of one's own country; it is more like the fellow-feeling that can develop among competitors in the same sporting event. There have been occasions when diplomats would find themselves more in agreement with each other than with their own governments, although this is more likely to occur in a multilateral context, like the United Nations, than in any particular capital. It is particularly likely to occur in difficult and drawn-out negotiations. The feeling could sometimes be summed up: "If only those SOBs at home would leave us alone, we could settle this thing overnight." Obviously this has its dangers and is another good reason for seeing that the decision-making authority remains at home, free from the seductive influences of group mechanics.

One result of the trade union spirit is that most people who've been in the business for any length of time have made some close friends among diplomats of other countries. Normally they would be from friendly countries but, subject to common sense, very comfortable personal relations have developed between representatives of countries that have little in common: Canadians and Moroccans, Australians and Afghanis and, occasionally, Americans and Russians — although this was rare in Cold War times. Even where official relations were anything but cosy, a sort of easy kidding relationship could develop. There was, for instance, a Soviet Ambassador in Ottawa with whom it was possible for those who dealt with him regularly to commiserate over the strange ways of the KGB ("the Centre," as the Moscow head office was known) on the one hand and the Special Branch of the RCMP on the other.

By the time John Diefenbaker had handed over office to L.B. Pearson, the Cold War had become, as one thought, a permanent fixture and the dominant factor in international life. Any issue that arose was treated for its relevance to the Cold War, and the only thing that anyone thought could replace that in their own lifetime was a hot war. Disarmament conferences went on interminably, more because no one wanted to bear the onus of breaking one up than out of any expectation that this was the road to peace. Successes in the field, few as they were, had more to do with economics than politics, which remained largely unaffected by the arms reductions that were achieved.

By the early sixties, hundreds of Canadian members of the armed forces and the Department had moved through Indochina's International Commissions for Supervision and Control (ICSC). Several had died there. Virtually every unmarried FSO, men and women alike, did at least one tour. Those who persisted in remaining single did more. At the beginning of the US intervention most Canadians in Indochina would have agreed that what the Americans were doing was good and proper, although there were always mutterings about the ways in which they were going about it. Some members of the military no doubt believed that Canada should have been there fighting but in the Department, at any rate, the "peacekeeping" role, frustrating and ineffective as it certainly was, was much preferable to work in the killing fields.

With the Cuban Crisis of October 1962 behind, the auguries for the coming years looked pretty good. "Peaceniks," flower children and violent Quebec nationalists had not yet become political factors. John XXIII was in Rome, Camelot was on the Potomac, the Kremlin was licking its Cuban wounds, the Middle East was quiescent and, at home, plans were under way for Canada's Centennial celebration. After a slow start, the Department was beginning to drum up participation for Expo 67 in Montreal, to be called "Man and His World." Such a sexist title was still thinkable.

5

Mike Pearson, PM

In April 1963, after ten years in the uncongenial wilderness of opposition, Mike Pearson led the Liberal Party back onto the government benches of Parliament and into the corridors of power — those high vaulted ones of the East Block where the cabinet officials and much of an expanded Department of External Affairs were still doing business. But Pearson's victory was not complete.

There is little evidence that the new Prime Minister's foreign operations were inhibited by the constraints of running a minority government or that they would have been conducted differently had his control over Parliament been more complete. It might be argued, however, that if a majority Pearson government had been less preoccupied with domestic politics, it might have been more active abroad. There is little evidence, however, to support the proposition.

Paul Martin, who had been Pearson's competitor for the leadership of the Liberals, became Secretary of State for External Affairs. For him it was a consolation prize worthy of the name. The new minister, affectionately and irreverently known in the Department as "Oom Paul," after Oom Paul Kruger of Boer War fame, was already a familiar figure in External Affairs. He had been on Canadian delegations to the old League of Nations before the war and was a regular member of our UN delegations while serving as Minister of Health and Welfare in the cabinet of Louis St. Laurent.

Notwithstanding the growing respect for Howard Green, the Department as a whole welcomed the change in government. It may not have been entirely out of a desire to see some hard decisions made after the Diefenbaker dithering, but that would have been reason enough. Perhaps it was thought that having "LBP" (as he used to initial his departmental papers) for Prime Minister would be the answer to its problems. If so, by the time Pearson retired five years later most could have agreed that while he travelled abroad a good deal and frequently spoke about foreign affairs, he never intervened with the Department's activities in any overt way. No External Affairs Minister, with the possible exception of Pearson himself, had more leeway than Paul Martin. Nevertheless, although Martin was in every sense his own man and left his personal stamp on the Department and its works, Pearson was also in the East Block and although his name was not always mentioned, everybody interested knew that when foreign policy decisions were made, LBP was not too far in the background.

The opening of the UN General Assembly in October marks the beginning of the international diplomatic year. In anticipation, every summer the Department held its annual hunt for Bold New Initiatives. If this was not a Martin innovation it was one he took a full part in; the cynics in External would not have hesitated to link it with Martin's continuing interest in giving a second meaning to the initials "PM," which he used on his departmental notes.

In the fall of 1963 Cyprus would not have appeared on anyone's list of issues that could require international attention. By December it was a full crisis and had moved to the top of the UN's agenda. The ancient Greek-Turkish antagonism that revolved around the fall of Constantinople in 1453 was still simmering in Cyprus. Just three years after Cyprus achieved its independence from Britain, the carefully cultivated resentments between its Greek and Turkish inhabitants exploded into a civil war. Animosities had been suppressed by British control and overshadowed by the Greek community's uprising against the British in the name of *enosis*, unification with Greece. With independence, the conflict took the familiar form — the right of the (Greek) majority to rule and the right of the (Turkish) minority to survive — but there were international complications.

By February of 1964, the Canadian High Commissioner, dually accredited from Israel, was sent from Tel Aviv to assess the situation with the possibility in mind that the UN might be asked to approve a peacekeeping force. Comparisons with UNEF, the operation that had earned Mike Pearson the Nobel Prize during the Suez Crisis, obviously were in the minds of those involved. But there were some disqualifying differences.

The Suez crisis arose in 1956 when the Egyptian President, Gamal Abdel Nasser, nationalized the historic Canal (the lifeline of Empire) then controlled by Britain and France. Pearson's idea of interposing United Nations forces between the parties in effect stopped a war that was actually in progress and had the potential to spread. While this was going on, the Hungarians were in open revolt and the Soviet army was on the march to suppress them. The possibility of the two conflagrations coming together was alarming.

In Cyprus, seven years later, what held most public attention were the mutual massacres, some gruesome pictures of which appeared on Cypriot greeting cards at the end of 1963. The fact that the two communities were being morally and materially supported by their Greek and Turkish homelands, both members of Nato, was a matter of serious concern to the Western alliance but it was not likely to lead to a general war. Still, there was another international aspect that gave the Cyprus problem some special urgency. The British airbase on Cyprus was the home of the "V" bombers whose mission in the event of war would have been to deliver atomic bombs to the southern parts of the Soviet Union. Cyprus was also known to have an active Communist Party with which the president of the republic, Archbishop Makarios III, had kept in touch since the recent end of the EOKA campaign led by "General Grivas" against British control. Here was a chance for the Soviet Union to fish in troubled and strategically important waters, an opportunity to harass Nato forces directed against the USSR. It would also keep the traditional discord between the two Nato allies alive, even to the point of hostilities between Greece and Turkey.

In principle, the UN did not intervene in internal conflicts, but in this case the secondary international implications were serious enough to bring about the creation of the United Nations Force in Cyprus (UNFICYP). The USSR, which rigidly opposed UN intervention in the internal affairs of its members, did not actually veto the arrangement but it was able to insist that the costs be met by voluntary contributions.

The Canadian military, who had been alerted to the possibility that their services might be required, were anxious to know just what would be involved. In March of 1964 a group of officers and supporting personnel were authorized to fly to Cyprus as a "reconnaissance party" to see what might be needed. While they were still en route, the UN and the Canadian Parliament had done their work so that by the time the group landed at Nicosia it had been designated the "advance party" for the newly created UNFICYP. The rest of the contingent followed swiftly to begin what was to become a thirty-year stay.

It was clear from the beginning that a speedy and peaceful settlement was not in the cards for this 500-year-old quarrel and that no Nobel Prizes were likely to come out of the Cyprus problem. It was reported in that way to Ottawa. Moreover, it was not long before it had become clear that far from making peace, UNFICYP, while it was saving lives, was also keeping the problem alive in spite of the best efforts of a series of UN mediators. At the root was the fact that the conflict was essentially a civil war in which the parties were supported by two outside states. Although the outside states and UNFICYP could ensure that there would be no settlement by the use of force, Greece, Turkey and the UN were all powerless to force the Greek and Turkish communities on Cyprus to modify their demands. This is what happens when a country like Greece or Turkey gives a veto over an aspect of its foreign policy to a group (like the Greek or Turkish community in Cyprus) that is outside its own jurisdiction. This divorce of authority from responsibility makes the larger partner a hostage to the smaller. As an added irony, the UN forces over the years became virtually incorporated into the local economy which, in turn, ensured that their withdrawal would be heavily resisted.

As early as 1965 this outcome could be foreseen. Moreover, as the role of the British "V" bombers stationed on Cyprus was taken over by intercontinental ballistic missiles, the island's strategic importance diminished accordingly. The Turkish invasion in July of 1974 divided the island into two separate political entities. Where once UNFICYP was seen as the protector of the Turkish community against the Greek majority, it then became the protector of the Greek community against the Turkish army. UNFICYP's role had been completely transformed. It had been set up to stabilize a situation that had threatened international peace and security. Soon after, however, its job became largely humanitarian, not primarily a Security Council matter, and hard to justify in terms of the costs involved for the international community.

Irony is a favourite form of military comment and as Canadian contingents changed it became the custom to greet the new arrivals with the lines from Shakespeare's *Othello*: "You are welcome, Sirs, to Cyprus." Very early on, at the ceremonial changing of the guard it was the custom for the departing commander to hand over to his relief a large bathroom sink plug and chain. No words were spoken.

Well before the creation of UNFICYP, the Department was learning that peacekeeping, in itself, had very little Holy Grail potential. It was a necessary part of the archetype of Middle Power but it was not a reliable source of influence, kudos or even of any great satisfaction.

Although Cyprus considers itself a part of Europe and not of the Middle East, for millennia it has been a meeting place for the two civilizations. Evidence of both are easy to see even for the casual visitor. Soon after Cyprus became an independent state within the Commonwealth in 1960, the Department appointed its then Ambassador to Israel, Margaret Meagher, to be concurrently High Commissioner to Cyprus. Most countries have problems with dual accreditation, and neither Israel nor Cyprus were entirely happy with the arrangement. The Department, however, persuaded its new High Commissioner to Cyprus that it would be a great place to get away from the pressures of Tel Aviv and Jerusalem.

By 1963, apart from sporadic shooting along the Golan Heights and in one or two other trouble spots, things had become fairly quiet on all of Israel's many fronts. John Diefenbaker, recently defeated and out of the Prime Minister's office, accepted an invitation to visit Israel that had been extended while he was in office. The Israelis took this in good grace and he was given the full treatment. While in office Diefenbaker had continued the policy toward Israel that he had inherited from his predecessor; when he left office, Pearson continued it. Canadian policy was easily stated: Israel had a right to exist and Canada would deal with Israel and the Arabs in an even-handed manner.

This apparently simple formula, in practice, was anything but. There were a number of factors at work. Each exerted its influence in different contexts but none was dominant. The first and probably the most important of these influences was the Canadian Jewish community: a large, close-knit, well-to-do, intelligent, highly motivated and politically active source of pressure. Not all Canadian Jews were Zionists, but the overwhelming majority were committed, not just to the continued existence, but to the welfare of the Jewish state.

A second factor at work in Canada's Middle East diplomacy was the long-standing commitment to the United Nations and to the concept of peacekeeping that put Canadian service people in all the peacekeeping and observer teams active in the area. If only because Israel's enemies usually outnumbered its friends in the UN, all of Israel's governments have, in differing degrees, mistrusted it. After making some strenuous efforts to gain support from Third World countries in particular, but without much success, and after seeing itself all but isolated on crucial votes in the General Assembly and in the Security Council, governments of Israel resisted giving the UN any role in matters affecting its own security. Occasionally this has put Canada, and some other countries, in the position of having to make a choice between the UN and Israel.

A third element was the Arab states and their oil wealth. Canada was one of relatively few countries where oil technology was up to world standards. Consequently, Canadian services were in demand in the Arab states, and the money was there to pay for them. Business opportunities in Arab countries were not confined to the oil sector by any means, but that was where the money came from to pay for goods, services and investments in Canada. So Canada had some solid economic interests in the Arab world which no Canadian government could ignore.

Small Arabic and Islamic elements in the Canadian population were quick to point out any real or imagined departure from the policy of even-handedness on the part of the government. They would be joined by otherwise disinterested persons who considered that the Palestinians had had a bad deal and needed friends such as themselves to help keep the Canadian government from tilting against them. There were others whose motives were simply anti-Jewish. Together they formed a segment of the population that could not be ignored. Pulled and pushed by this mix of forces, all Canadian governments have wobbled. The UN has been supported against Israel (concerning the status of Jerusalem); Israel has been supported against the UN and against the Arabs (in objecting to intemperate language in resolutions that would otherwise have been acceptable); the Arabs have been supported against Israel (in resolutions about frontiers and the future of the Palestinians).

A few generalizations may be possible. Canadian governments have been, as they should be, highly responsive to popular and political pressures in this area and have tried their best to make defensible decisions based on the principle of even-handedness. Both sides deny that any Canadian government has been really even-handed and, to this, the pro-Israel side may also add that almost any given attempt to strike a balance between, say, Israel and the Palestinians could undermine the security of the Jewish state to which Canada is committed. It would be surprising if Canada ever had or ever would consciously support any move that threatened the security of Israel, although both sides could argue the contrary because security depends entirely on the point from which it is viewed.

There's also a problem with the very concept of even-handedness, which suggests a baseball umpire who doesn't worry too much about calling balls and strikes accurately so long as they come out even in the end. Canada's commitment to the security of the state of Israel, according to the pro-Arab side, prejudged everything, particularly since the pro-Israel side claimed that any unfavourable decision threatened Israel's security. In spite of never being achieved to the satisfaction of those most concerned, even-handedness was probably as reasonable a policy aim as the Canadian situation permitted.

In 1963 the official Canadian position was that the State of Israel was the one described by the United Nations resolution (in whose drafting Mr Justice Ivan Rand of Canada had played a significant part) which was miraculously passed with Soviet approval in November of 1947. That resolution said among other things that Palestine, the old League of Nations mandated territory, should be divided into a Jewish state, an Arab state and an international *corpus separatum*, the city of Jerusalem. The Canadian position was that this concept was not invalidated by the subsequent rejection of the UN decision by the Arabs nor by the wars waged and lost by them after that. The State of Israel was recognized but the frontiers claimed by Israel were not. The government of Israel subsequently declared Jerusalem to be its capital, but Canada, along with a number of other countries including notably the United States, kept their embassies in Tel Aviv so as not to prejudge the "ownership" of Jerusalem.

It may not have been mere coincidence that the period of relative stability between the mid-fifties and the mid-sixties was also a time when Israel was led by an extraordinary group of exceptionally open-minded and forward-looking people, mostly with European or American backgrounds: David Ben-Gurion, Levi Eshkol, Golda Meir, Abba Eban, the Weizmanns, the Herzogs. Although these people had little success in coming to an understanding with Israel's neighbours they freely acknowledged that the future of Israel depended on doing just that.

The Department's introduction to Middle East politics took place early on. In 1947 when the United Nations passed its miraculous resolution and the State of Israel was declared, Elizabeth MacCallum was the Department's only real Middle East expert. As an Arabist, she was clearly predisposed to sympathize with the Arab position in the UN debates that led to the creation of Israel. She was also convinced that the head of her own delegation, Mike Pearson, had missed some broad signals being sent out by some Arab delegates that a compromise might be possible. She knew that these signals may well have been merely tactical and intended to delay, but she thought they should have been explored anyway. When they were not she scribbled a note and passed it to Pearson saying that the Middle East was now in for "forty years" of war. She probably thought it unnecessary to add that it would be a biblical forty years.

MacCallum's influence has been said to have biased the Department toward the Arab point of view more or less ever since. Two things should be noted. The first is that although Elizabeth was a much-loved figure in the Department, nobody ever succeeded in making that kind of lasting impression on External's people and even less on matters of policy. Moreover, it was virtually a condition of employment to work loyally in applying policies regardless of personal opinions. Either that, or you quit. The democratic process itself depended on this. Consequently, if there was a long-term bias in Canadian external policy (as there might well have been) it would be too simple to blame the Department or anyone in it without recognizing the decisive role of the government itself. Canada's Middle East policy, as already mentioned, involved many domestic political considerations, and where they applied even the most objective views offered by External were not necessarily accepted. Members of the government would quickly have recognized obviously biased ones, particularly if they disagreed with them. They would have given them very short shrift indeed.

Canadians who worked in Israel during this period, with hardly an exception, were captivated by the country and the people and, most of all, by what had been achieved by the Israelis. Most non-Israelis who have lived in Israel would agree that admiration was not always enough. Attitudes were very important to Israelis, who seemed to respond almost instinctively to whether the visitor was sympathetic or the reverse on any given issue. Neutrality was treated with unconcealed scepticism. This could make it difficult for foreign diplomats whose obligations were to their own government and to its policies and priorities, few of which would coincide with those of any other state.

Whatever anyone thought of Israel's foreign policies, there was no disagreement about the calibre of its diplomats at that time. Their combination of firmness and flexibility made anyone interested in peace and stability in the Middle East wish that the other side had been as well equipped.

In December of 1967, as the Centennial Year was coming to its end, Mike Pearson made his anticipated announcement of his intention to retire. Even before that, cartoonists had been having a good time depicting Paul Martin or Mitchell Sharp trying on running shoes. After he announced his intention, Pearson was not exactly a lame duck — he still had the power to be a kingmaker — but he was no longer the dominant factor in the government.

During his periods in public office Pearson, more than anyone else, was identified with public positions and actions that, long after he left office, were still being linked to Canada on the international scene. As Prime Minister he had authorized the Canadian representative on the International Commission in Indochina, Blair Seaborn, to carry a message from Washington to Hanoi telling the North Vietnamese that the United States would extend its bombing to the populated centres of the north unless there was some progress toward a ceasefire. Then, as a Nobel laureate, and inescapably as Prime Minister, Pearson criticized the United States for going ahead and carrying out its threat. There were Canadians who deplored the delivery of this message, which they regarded as an act of subservience to the United States. On the other hand the American President, Lyndon Johnson, among others, heartily resented Pearson's criticism of US actions in Indochina.

In Canada, critics paid little attention to the fact that the delivery of the American message to Hanoi also allowed Canada to pass along the North Vietnamese reaction to the planned bombing and the view that it would not have the desired effect. Canada's willingness to help the United States in its Vietnam difficulty was well understood outside the country, just as our ability to take contrary positions was appreciated.

It was also during Pearson's leadership that Canada took the first step that was later to lead to the rehabilitation of the effective government of China and its occupation of the seat reserved for China at the United Nations. The occasion was the 1966 annual Albanian resolution calling for the seating of the People's Republic of China. As usual, the resolution was couched in insulting language that was in itself too objectionable to support. In previous years Canada, along with the rest of the Western allies, had voted against the Albanian initiative. Under the active leadership of Paul Martin, the Canadian delegation in New York, and indeed Canadian representatives in many other capitals, had pursued many variations on ways in which the rulers of the most populous country on earth could be represented at the UN. These included the so-called Two China approach, which would give the People's Republic of China one seat and the Taiwan regime another. All the efforts had failed on opposition from one side or the other. So, when the Albanian resolution came up at the UN General Assembly in 1966, the Canadian delegation broke with its allies and instead of voting against it, Canada abstained. The scene was set for the next phase which followed the election of Pearson's successor in 1968.

There have been few important international issues on which Canada has disagreed publicly with the United States to compare with China. The Chinese rejection of the Chiang Kai-shek regime was a very sore point with the Americans, who had a warm spot for China. The United States believed that it had opened the doors of China to the world and that it had a special sort of relationship with that country. Then suddenly China had gone communist and Chinese "volunteers" were sent to Korea where they killed large numbers of American soldiers. American resentments of Peking were stronger than most Canadians were able to believe.

Years before he became Prime Minister, Pearson had forecast that the days of an "easy and automatic" relationship between Canada and the United States were over. In a sense he helped fulfil his own prophecy, notably when in April of 1965 he made a speech in the United States criticizing the American government's conduct of the war in Vietnam. No one should have been surprised that John Diefenbaker was unloved in Washington but it was ironic that Pearson, with so many American connections and assumed by many Americans to be one of their own, should have found himself in the same position. The late sixties were touchy times; in those circumstances, telling a neighbour what you thought of him was not likely to have constructive results.

The United States was not alone in having divisive internal problems, as General de Gaulle would remind Canadians. Nothing makes the diplomat's job easier and more pleasant than to represent the government of a country that is sure of itself, knows where it wants to go and how it proposes to get there. But representing a divided country is very tough. First there is the business of having to reassure interested foreigners that the country is not going to vanish from the map. This takes up time that would otherwise go into more productive things. But, more important are the lingering doubts that remain in the minds of foreigners who make decisions, whether business or political. The activities of the Quebec separatists in the second half of the 1960s did take the gilt off the Centennial and even Expo 67. Foreign visitors, heads of state and members of royal families who came to admire carried home with them questions as well as answers.

Even though 1967 was a high point in many ways, the future of the country was being questioned abroad. General de Gaulle's balcony speech and the Canadian government's reaction to it left impressions that continued to trouble the Department's agents abroad for years to come.

Before Mike Pearson retired in early 1968 the Department, like the country itself, was looking over his shoulder, the way some people do at diplomatic receptions, to see who was coming next. Internal disunity was growing and the government's agenda was vague. All of Canada was marking time, awaiting change and hoping for the best.

The Age of Reasons
1968–1984

6

Enter Trudeau, Frowning

"The best" simply had to be Pierre Elliott Trudeau. He had been persuaded to run for the leadership of the Liberal Party, which he won after four ballots in April of 1968. He went on to lead the party to electoral victory in June the same year.

The new Prime Minister seemed to have been made to External's specifications and it was generally believed that he came with LBP's personal stamp of approval. Doubters were few, although they did exist. Everyone else in the Department was sure the country had found its saviour in this enlightened, intelligent, well-educated, articulate (in both languages) new leader. It was taken for granted that he would be well disposed toward the like-minded folk of External Affairs. Pierre Trudeau never said anything to disabuse them, although, in retrospect, he gave some pretty clear signals. Ultimately his attitude toward the Department led to its downgrading and to the weakening of the one group within the government that could have helped him achieve the sort of recognition on the world stage that he actively sought during his last years in office.

Underlings, or "subalterns," as General de Gaulle referred to second-stringers, are notoriously wrong-headed in interpreting the motives of the great persons they serve, tending either to idolize or underrate their masters, but they are well placed to see what is going on. No one has yet been able to say without inviting powerful contradiction that they knew what motivated Pierre Trudeau. His actions and their effects, being on the record, are less open to debate.

In January of 1969 one of the early meetings between the new Prime Minister and some of the leading lights of External took place in London during the meeting of the Commonwealth Heads of Government at Marlborough House, where he made his famous bannister slide. The Department thought the occasion a good opportunity for Trudeau to meet the heads of our European diplomatic missions. They gathered at Canada House, with Marcel Cadieux, then still Undersecretary, presiding. There began a cranky discussion on the state of the world, each head of post trying to make the most of his or her own job. There had been rumours of changes and no doubt all present thought they had to justify their existences anew. Whatever the reason, the results were not comfortable even before the Prime Minister came to speak to the group. He did not stay long but he was frank.

He began by saying how very impressed he was by the array of talent he saw before him and how much respect he had for the Department and all its works. However (and it was a long however), he had some young friends in the Department who did not share this high opinion of their bosses. He created the impression that he intended to find a way of seeing that all those bright ideas that had been trapped in the gravity of External could escape. Here was an attractive, smiling, urbane, articulate and very knowledgeable person who also happened to be the Prime Minister saying, it seemed, exactly what was on his mind. The impression he left on some of his listeners was tremendous, particularly on those who thought theirs would be among the ideas he would want.

That evening, at Upper Brook Street, which was the residence of the Canadian High Commissioner, Charles and Sylvia Ritchie gave a reception for the heads of mission and the wives who had come to London with them. The *chers collègues* were on their very worst behaviour, exuding professional charm even on each other and manoeuvring casually, with practised skill, to make their number with the Prime Minister. Any doubts Mr Trudeau may have had about External's brightest and best could have been confirmed then and there.

Mitchell Sharp was the new Prime Minister's choice as Secretary of State for External Affairs. Although Sharp was the formal link between the government and the political leadership, Ivan Head, the new Foreign Affairs Advisor in the Prime Minister's Office, was generally regarded as Trudeau's personal source of ideas and information about External Affairs. The Department's business was conducted through the usual channels — Undersecretary, to Mitchell Sharp, to cabinet—but it was widely assumed that there was an informal channel through which individuals in the Department could make contact with the PMO.

Ivan had served in External between 1960 and 1968, some of which time was spent on educational leave. However, he was not a member of the Department when he became Foreign Affairs

Advisor to the Prime Minister. He was accordingly resented as the first non-External person to have such responsibility in the PMO. After a few short years in academe he had leapt ahead of his seniors to the point where journalists were referring to him, rather than Mitchell Sharp, as the real foreign minister. Indeed, Ivan did perform some functions on behalf of the Prime Minister that might, in other circumstances, have been performed by or under the direction of the Secretary of State for External Affairs, but he was extremely careful to deny any such role for himself.

Moreover, because of Ivan's connections within the Department it was suspected that he was doing end-runs around the hierarchy. Ideas solicited by the Prime Minister from the lower echelons could, via Ivan, escape the knives of Killers' Row, as the corridor that accommodated the assistant undersecretaries was known. That was not necessarily all bad, but it could cause chaos if one kind of advice was coming up the bureaucratic net, via the Undersecretary and Minister, and something different was going straight to the PMO without running the usual gauntlet. Within six months of taking office it was becoming clear that the Prime Minister was not going to get anything like all of his advice on foreign affairs from External. At least some people in the Department consoled themselves by arguing that if there had to be an Ivan Head, Ivan was the best Ivan Head as the Department could hope for.

Trudeau's relationship with External was soon to be complicated by a different subject of prime ministerial attention, his interest in the machinery of government in the form of "management by objectives" and in the name of which External's primacy in the foreign field would be diminished.

In retrospect it is clear that Pierre Trudeau, from the beginning of his tenure as Prime Minister, had had very little time for the Department. Given the state of its administrations, it is easy to sympathize with him at a superficial level. On the other hand it was the Department doing what it did best that made it possible for Trudeau to make his first significant impression on the international community through the establishment of relations with the People's Republic of China. The skills the Department, working as a team, had developed during its Golden Age, when it was helping to create and then act out the role of Middle Power, were still there. As it turned out they were present in sufficient strength to give reality to the Prime Minister's 1968 election promise that he was going to help bring the real China into the family of nations from which it had so long been excluded.

One day in September of 1968 a diplomatic bag arrived in the Canadian Embassy in Stockholm from the Department, containing a dark red Accopress binder holding documents, on legal-size paper, an inch thick. The covering letter said that the government had decided to begin negotiation with representatives of the People's Republic of China (PRC) with a view to recognizing it as the legal government of China. The initial contact was to be made in Stockholm, a neutral capital in which Beijing and Canada both had embassies. No contact was to be made until after the impending election in the United States was over and the new president had taken office. This was to avoid the possibility that the Canadian initiative might become an issue in the American election.

The book represented the work of many people in Ottawa whose responsibilities would be affected by the anticipated change, including functionaries in Citizenship and Immigration, the RCMP, Finance, and Trade and Commerce. They had all been through much the same process many times before and some of their contributions were no doubt updates of earlier versions.

Like any foreign ministry, the Department had been unhappy not to have relations with a government as important as the government in Beijing, which spoke for a quarter of the world's population. Indeed the Canadian government had been on the verge of extending recognition when the Korean War broke out in mid-1950. The Canadian idea of a "decent interval" between the cessation of hostilities and diplomatic relations was much shorter than the Americans' notion and for years after the war was over, the word from Washington remained the same: it would be taken amiss if Canada moved to rehabilitate a country whose soldiers had killed so many Americans so recently. It was beside the point that these same Chinese and their Korean allies had also killed some 300 Canadians in the same conflict.

It had continued to bother Ottawa that the China seat at the UN should be occupied by a rump of a government holed up in Taiwan behind the protection of an American fleet. Successive governments under Diefenbaker and Pearson had pressed the issue of Chinese representation at New York and, indeed, Diefenbaker's pursuit of the matter led to the famous Eisenhower rebuke: Canada should make up its mind whether it wanted Communist China or the United States in the UN; it couldn't have both. That was discouraging but it was not the end of the matter. When Paul Martin became minister he returned to the charge with fresh proposals, including variants of the "Two China" solution, one seat for "the mainland" and one for Taiwan. In the meantime, as mentioned earlier, Canada loyally went along with the Americans whenever it came to a vote in the UN. Not until late in 1966 did we break ranks on the perennial Albanian resolution to seat the PRC and switch from a negative vote to an abstention. Albania's resolutions were always couched in such offensive language that it was easy to vote against them simply on those grounds, but in 1966 Canada held its nose and abstained.

Throughout the period 1955 to 1966 the Department may have been divided on how much weight US sensitivity should carry against the conviction that China ought to be brought into the UN family. The Department was less divided on the merits of the recognition of China itself. It has been alleged, and perhaps with a grain of truth, that External's attitude on the China question was influenced by the half-dozen or so "mishkids," children of Canadian missionaries who had served there. One or two (especially Chester Ronning) were active proponents of recognition, but most of them were neither in a position to exert influence nor interested in doing so. The conventional wisdom in the Department was simply that the government in Beijing was in effective control of virtually all of China and there was no reasonable prospect of that changing. It was not a matter of approval but of realism.

So the Department would have been neither shocked nor displeased when Pierre Trudeau during his first general election campaign, in early 1968, declared: "Our aim will be to recognize the People's Republic of China government as soon as possible and to enable that government to occupy the seat of China in the United Nations, taking into account that there is a separate government in Taiwan." Paul Martin could not have said it better.

Although it is true that Trudeau's declaration of intent was a continuation of a long-standing Canadian objective, the plan put forward under his direction represented an entirely new approach. Instead of trying to manoeuvre the United Nations (and the United States along with it) into doing the realistic thing, under Trudeau it was decided to reverse the order of business and to start by doing what lay within Canada's own power to do. It would deal directly with Beijing itself. It was a greater change in the way Canada had traditionally operated than most people realized at the time. Under its new leadership, Canada had moved away from the multilateral approach which had led nowhere and was daring to do what it could by itself on a bilateral level.

The outcome was that in October of 1970 the "Canadian formula" was accepted by both sides in Stockholm. The agreement reached differed in one significant respect from what had been enunciated by Trudeau in 1968. The Trudeau statement had clearly implied recognition of two Chinas, but very early in the negotiations this was seen as a non-starter and that condition was dropped. In the final accord the government of Canada recognized the government in Beijing "as the sole legal government of China."

What had taken so long in reaching agreement was the Chinese demand that Taiwan be explicitly included in the territory of the PRC that was being recognized. The Canadian compromise took the form of two statements. The first said: "The Chinese Government affirms that Taiwan is an inalienable part of the territory of the People's Republic of China." The second followed immediately but as a separate paragraph. It said: "The Canadian Government takes note of this position of the Chinese Government."

To leave no room for misunderstanding, the minister, Mitchell Sharp, who had played the traditional role as the responsible cabinet minister throughout the negotiation, made a statement in the House of Commons. In it he said that the Canadian statement meant that Canada was aware of the Chinese position on Taiwan, "and we realize the importance they attach to it, but we have no comment to make one way or the other." To avoid any nasty surprises, the Embassy in Stockholm had taken the precaution of letting the Chinese see a copy of the statement the minister intended to make. The Chinese apparently decided that they, too, need only take note of the Canadian position and no comments were made.

When Canada's intention to seek mutual recognition with the PRC was announced it created quite an international stir. Before Mitchell Sharp announced in the House of Commons on February 10, 1969, that negotiations had begun, our Ambassador to Washington, Ed Ritchie, went to the State Department to tell them what was coming. He was sternly advised of the foolishness of such a breach in Western solidarity.

The Japanese had noted the references to China that had been made during the election campaign and they had followed what we were doing with particular interest and persistence. Although the Japanese were not at all anxious to do any pioneering on this subject, they did not intend to be too far behind the leader, whoever it might be. They, too, had to be kept in the picture. While our own negotiations were under way, both Italy and Belgium had made approaches of their own, but for a variety of reasons they failed. Obviously, there was also great interest in Nato.

Twenty months after the first contact, when the Embassy in Washington informed the State Department that a deal had been struck in Stockholm, our messenger was told in comparatively mild terms that Canada had made a serious mistake. Nothing more. In the interval Richard Nixon had established himself in the White House and had brought Henry Kissinger with him. A reappraisal of American policies in Asia beginning with Vietnam was under way. The Canadian initiative was, therefore, no longer a betrayal but merely an inconvenience and, it seems in retrospect, an awkward anticipation of what the new American administration itself had in mind. If Canada had in some way forced the pace we had also made a valuable reconnaissance into unknown territory and had generally prepared the ground in a way that would make a fundamental change in American policy more acceptable inside and outside the United States.

There was another important factor in American calculations. The United States could not be seen to fail one of its oldest international friends and allies, the Nationalist Chinese. The United States was bound to strive, if not to keep Taipei as the capital of all of China or sitting in the China seat in the Security Council, then at least to keep Nationalist China as a member of the United Nations. This was the situation when the annual Albanian resolution to seat Beijing and throw out Taipei came before the General Assembly in late October of 1971.

When all the voting was over and the battle to keep Taiwan in the UN had been lost, the anger of the United States, which some had expected to be directed toward Canada, was directed primarily at the UN itself. There was a debate in Congress about continued US involvement with the UN; William Rogers, the Secretary of State, made a statement to the effect that the United States should take a fresh look at the extent of American financial support of the UN, to which it was then paying more than its fair share. Rogers "hoped" the UN would not be weakened by Taiwan's expulsion and said the State Department would be making it clear to those countries who he said had "told us one thing and did another" that "we don't particularly like that." Canada could not be included in that category.

Commenting on the outcome of the UN vote, the President's press secretary objected publicly to the "shocking demonstration" of "undisguised glee" after the vote had been announced and said that Nixon himself had found it offensive and undignified. There had indeed been an anti-American flavour to the outburst in the General Assembly when the results of the voting had become known. The Canadian delegation, headed by Yvon Beaulne, although pleased by the outcome, remained seated, dignified and impassive throughout.

There was, however, one Canadian attempt to josh the Americans. While the debate was taking place, it had been announced that Dr Kissinger was then in Shanghai talking officially to the government whose recognition the United States was opposing in New York. A note was circulated in the Canadian delegation at the General Assembly which read "I wonder where's Kissinger now?" It eventually reached Beaulne who, after reading it, took the note over to the American delegation bench and left it on the desk in front of its leader, one George Bush. Bush showed no sign of having been joshed.

The reaction was hardly surprising. The American delegation had pulled out every stop to keep the PRC from ousting Taiwan from the United Nations and, having failed, there was nothing to be graceful about. Although the Department certainly was aware of the strength of American feeling on this issue and no doubt had advised the government accordingly, and although the American factor did affect the timing of the Chinese initiative, this did not prevent Trudeau's government from acting.

Events justified their decision. Less than thirteen months after the Canadian negotiation had been successfully completed, the People's Republic of China occupied China's permanent seat in the UN Security Council. According to Huang Hua, the Chinese Ambassador in Ottawa who was sent to New York to occupy the seat, the change had occurred at least a year before anyone in Beijing had expected it could.

Only the force of Pierre Trudeau's personality and his determination to deal with this matter made it possible. To him also must go credit for cutting a hoary old Gordian knot by deciding that Canada would go it alone where previous governments had tried to deal with the China question as a member of the Western team.

And he did it in spite of well-known American sensitivity and perhaps some cautionary notes from the Department about not irritating the United States on an issue of such marginal national importance to Canada as China.

Thus ended a process that had been a minor obsession within External Affairs since the outbreak of the Korean War and a more widely based Canadian concern that the most populous country in the world was not represented at the UN. The timing was fortuitous in that no one could have known for sure that the Cultural Revolution had just about run its course when the Prime Minister made his speech in April of 1968. Certainly if Beijing had not been ready for change, no initiative could have succeeded.

Once the government gave the Department its instruction to proceed, External did its part with patience and skill. It was able to maintain sufficient secrecy to keep the Chinese negotiators from being embarrassed at home and yet our friends and allies with special interests and, indeed, Parliament itself were all kept generally informed. When it was concluded, the damage to our relations with the United States was minimal. The United Nations was strengthened and the international community was impressed by Canada's independence and vision.

The negotiation was a textbook example of how governments should use their diplomats: an imaginative decision was made at the political level; the objections of the experts (in this case over the probable American reaction) were considered and overruled; the experts then produced the necessary background papers putting the proposal into its historical context; and the implications for the future were discussed. A negotiating procedure was thoroughly prepared, giving starting positions and some fall-backs, a loose timetable and a venue. After cabinet approval, the plan was handed back to Secretary of State for External Affairs Mitchell Sharp for implementation. There were regular reports to cabinet via its Committee on External Affairs and Defence, where fresh or revised instructions were discussed and approved, but there was no evidence of further involvement by the Prime Minister's Office.

The China negotiation had been begun, conducted and successfully concluded before Trudeau's managerial revolution got fully under way and yet it is hard to think of anything that the Trudeau government achieved on the international scene in the years it was in office to match the significance of this early initiative.

Although the Chinese negotiations had been conducted under the old rules of departmental responsibility, the government's intention to change the way the Department operated had been made clear well before the Chinese initiative had been concluded. Even the most conservative member of the Department could not deny that there was a need for changes in the way it operated. In spite of the obvious links between the Department's administration and the policies it managed, administration had always been a poor step-child and tended either to be left to the clerical staff or to be done reluctantly by Foreign Service personnel as a matter of painful duty. The mainstream people would decide, with little or no administrative input, what they wanted to do and then leave it to the administrative staff to find the resources needed to do it. Budgeting was a mystical process more related to getting money out of the Treasury Board than it was to a systematic projection of operations for the coming year. This was not entirely External's fault. The financial controllers' short-term views on, for instance, capital spending did not encourage realism. This sort of *ad hoc*-ery was about to change.

It began with the new government's determination to write its own foreign policy untrammelled by past thinking and, certainly, by past operating methods. Besides a fresh new approach to foreign policy, there was to be a whole new philosophy of government called "management by objectives."

During the fall of 1969 and the following winter, Geoff Murray, an FSO who had once been an aide to Dag Hammarskjold, and Bill Barton, an FSO with a scientific background and a future ambassador to the UN, had been working on the fresh statement of foreign policy principles and guidelines demanded by the new government. The product was published in 1970 as a series of booklets collectively called *Foreign Policy for Canadians*.

The process of preparing this overview of everything was extremely difficult for the Department and particularly for Marcel Cadieux. As an Undersecretary in the tradition of Norman Robertson, Marcel was being asked to question all the assumptions he had taken as basic throughout his entire career. When the answers that were first produced failed to meet with the approval of the PMO, they came back with the request that the Department try again. According to Cadieux, when the Department's offerings were sent back there were few suggestions of what should replace them.

When he asked for some indication of what was wanted he was told, "you're the experts, you tell us."

The people who produced *Foreign Policy for Canadians* entered into the spirit of the new order and eventually delivered what was required of them with great difficulty and after much internal and external debate. There was a bad moment when the press got wind of one version which presented Canadian foreign policy as a multicoloured graphic in the form of a hexagon. Perhaps as a result of some horse-laughs from the media, the graphic was not produced with the final publication. The omission was a pity because it was a remarkable illustration of the rigorously logical process that characterized the Prime Minister's approach to government. In the end, six booklets were produced covering all the important aspects of Canadian foreign policy save one — the American relationship. Critics said it was *Hamlet* without the Prince of Denmark; defenders argued that the American fact permeated everything and was therefore incorporated in all the other parts. The deficiency, however, was soon to be made up.

There were some curious contradictions in the government's thinking about the technique of making foreign policy. It argued that foreign policy comes out of the internal interests of the state concerned. Scant attention was paid to the external forces that severely limit any country's ability to get what it wants from the rest of the world. It was as if the government believed it could do as it wished in the pursuit of Canada's objectives. In fact, for a smallish country, foreign influences are often, if not usually, more important than internal considerations when operating in the foreign environment. Sometimes they dictate the domestic policy. For a country like Israel, for instance, external considerations virtually set the agenda.

The new Canadian government, however, gave the impression that it was within its power to create a brand new foreign policy, as if the underlying factors of the nation's life, its national interests — which had not changed — could produce a wide range of equally valid options. The government could then choose the policy that suited it best. Changes in foreign policies are, of course, possible, as the Chinese initiative had shown. Nonetheless, in the case of China there was the winding up of the Cultural Revolution and a new and, in its way, radical government in Washington, two external factors that made a new policy possible and timely.

The best known statement in the introductory booklet of *Foreign Policy for Canadians* was a disavowal of the role of "helpful fixer." The main purpose was no doubt to stress that there was a new man in charge and he had a different outlook from his predecessor. Pearson fans saw it as a slight, but new prime ministers usually do go out of their way to make the point that a different and better regime is now in charge. Moreover, the expression "helpful fixer" suggested Trudeau's distaste for fuzzy thinking and soft options. Nevertheless when the occasion arose, in the Trudeau as in the Pearson eras, the Canadian government rarely, if ever, declined to take on a "helpful fixer" job. The trouble was that Canadians saw themselves as "helpful fixers"; that was one of those internal "givens" which do influence a foreign policy without too much regard for who heads the government.

Foreign Policy for Canadians was the Department's first ever attempt to present a clear, consistent and across-the-board statement of what the country's external interests were. Policy statements had, until now, been confined to specific issues and usually related to a situation that had actually arisen. These booklets were an attempt to anticipate needs and adopt positions based on principles worked out in advance rather than to rely on reactive *ad hoc*-ery. The idea was bold and new, but in the end, *Foreign Policy for Canadians* presented few substantial departures from past policies. There were new rationales and new approaches but the end results were familiar. Attempts were made to change long-established policy, for instance in the matter of Canada's military presence in Europe, but it can be argued that they were mistaken and damaging to Canada's interests. Eventually they had to be revised.

For two years after the new policy review was published, the focal point of Canadian foreign policy remained unexamined. In the final analysis, it was how Trudeau intended to deal with the United States that would say the most about the new Prime Minister's view of Canada's place in the outside world.

Canadians and their southern neighbours have been of more or less constant interest to each other since the time when both were ruled from London. The United States was on the agenda of the Department when it came into existence in 1909 and as long as the two countries remain separate entities they will continue to be of interest, or concern, to each other. The common frontier took a while being drawn but once decided it has varied only in minor details. Unlike most frontiers, our so-called border never made military or economic sense. Its meaning derives from the differences that are found on either side; originally between New France and New England, later deepened and strengthened by the influx of the United Empire Loyalists and institutionalized by a Canadian Confederation based on the ideal of peace, order and good government, as compared to the other based on life, liberty and the pursuit of happiness. The claims of society were stressed in the north; those of the individual dominated in the south. Since Confederation, Canada, in its crab-like way, has created its own North American alternative, which has been protected and advanced by an effective diplomacy that was evolved largely for that purpose. The Department developed special skills in anticipating reactions in the United States and avoiding confrontations with its powerful neighbour while ultimately relying on an American sense of fair play toward the normally placid underdog. The great test of any Canadian government in the area of foreign affairs has been how it has maintained this relationship, a nice balance between independence and accommodation. This was a matter that got a good deal of attention in the late sixties and early seventies. On his first trip to the United States as Prime Minister, Trudeau made his now famous analysis: "Living next to you is in some ways like sleeping with an elephant. No matter how friendly and even-tempered the beast, if I can call it that, one is affected by every twitch and grunt ..."

In 1972, two years after *Foreign Policy for Canadians* appeared, the government produced a statement on the Canada–United States relationship, not as an additional booklet in the foreign policy collection but as a special issue of *International Perspectives*, then the Department's quasi-independent organ of opinion on international affairs. It was entitled *Canada-U.S. Relations: Options for the Future* and was signed by Mitchell Sharp as minister. The person responsible for putting it together was Klaus Goldschlag, an incisive thinker and writer, who was then head of the USA Division in the Department.

The article presented three possible courses for Canada in its dealings with the United States. The First Option was to "maintain more or less our present relationship"; i.e., to continue to let economic forces determine the future. This course, the paper predicted, "would bring Canada more closely into the US orbit" and have much the same result as the Second Option. That was to "move deliberately toward closer integration with the United States." After examining the implications of this second course, the paper concluded that an economy-driven move to come closer to the United States would lead inevitably to political as well as economic integration and that "might be expected to generate opposition in Canada," as the paper so dryly put it.

The Third Option, which was adopted along with the name, was "to pursue a comprehensive long-term strategy" to hold the line at the existing degree of American involvement in the Canadian economy in terms of markets and sources of supply and of capital. To achieve this result Canada would have to mount a strong campaign to diversify markets and sources of investment and direct the future expansion of the Canadian economy so that the American share would grow with it but not increase in relative terms, as compared with other countries. This presupposed some very hard work by the Department of Industry, Trade and Commerce which, by bitter experience, knew just how difficult it could be to get Canadian exporters to move into new markets.

In 1974 Japan was a key element in the Third Option policy. Europe was busy trying to coalesce and for other reasons was not too interested in Canada, so if Canada was to try to hold American involvement in the Canadian economy at its existing level, much of what we required by way of markets and investment for growth would have to come from Japan. The Department's job was to keep the United States reassured while arousing the interest of Japanese investors and traders.

At this strategic juncture the Department was being pressed to reorganize itself both in its own operations and as a part of the general rationalization of the process of government. It would be wrong to blame the failure of the Third Option on the government's decision to announce a bold new policy in our relations with the United States and simultaneously tinker with the machinery that was supposed to implement the policy. But it certainly didn't help.

That failure was due to large number of factors. First there was the absence of a clearly established "centre of responsibility," to use a phrase current at the time. For the plan to have succeeded, a co-ordinated multidepartmental worldwide effort would have to have been organized and managed centrally with firm and continuous support from the Prime Minister. For instance, the government's inability to interest the Japanese was to some extent due to a current Japanese belief that Canada was part of the US economic hinterland. At that time the Japanese were reluctant to move in on American "turf" because they thought doing so might raise the ire of the United States, which they were not yet ready to confront. Later, the Japanese got over this fear, no doubt with Canada's help, but it was too little and too late for the Third Option.

At the time, too, the government, while interested in attracting foreign investment, was opposed to allowing foreign investors to direct the products of their Canadian investments to the markets of their choice. The Japanese were in search of assured supplies of raw materials and would not invest in a Canadian resource industry unless they were sure that its product would go to Japan. This Canadian policy changed too, but again too late for the Third Option.

The quietus was administered by the Canadian business community, which was clearly not interested in fighting for new markets and new sources of investment and in dealing with strange languages and customs, when the old familiar markets and investors were still willing to do business at the old stand in the United States. This, when combined with the government's lack of committment to its own policy, left the Third Option a dead letter almost from its inception.

To top it all off, Washington disliked this new policy intensely and on every possible occasion presented it as an attempt to cut back on American participation in the Canadian economy rather than to keep the American share of our growth at its existing level. American representatives dismissed departmental attempts to justify the Third Option as pro-Canadian rather than anti-American as mere hairsplitting. Although there were elements in Canadian society that objected strongly to the Third Option, there was surprisingly little debate about the proposal. Within the Department, it simply seemed self-evident that Canadians would want to keep American influences in Canada under control. But when it came to implementation of the policy, American resentments, added to a lack of leadership and bureaucratic and business inertia, brought this bold new initiative to nothing.

The Third Option was, at the time, only one of many sources of American unhappiness with Canada. The Prime Minister's style and his inability to be overly impressed by persons or things must have upset the leadership in Washington. In the realm of ideas, as Joe Clark once observed, Trudeau looked more toward Europe (he might have added Asia) than to the United States. As Prime Minister, Trudeau dealt with most people in the same slightly off-hand way that must have seemed to verge on disrespect, particularly to

American presidents. A man who could slide down the bannister at Marlborough House or do a pirouette after calling on the Queen was clearly not reliable, not at all the good grey Canadian who could be taken for granted.

So Pierre Trudeau and his policies were something new in the Canada–US equation. On the one hand there had been Canadians who talked of "no truck nor trade with the Yankees" and on the other there had been those who regarded the 49th parallel as a figment of the imagination and who considered themselves to be as good Americans as anyone south of that artificial line. Americans had been accustomed to the aloof self-righteousness of a Diefenbaker, the deference of a Mackenzie King, the rumpled friendliness of a Pearson — but a cool and detached Pierre Trudeau with a sharp mind and philosophical bent could only raise dark suspicions in the likes of Richard Nixon and incomprehension in Gerald Ford.

Perhaps unconsciously, the Department took the Prime Minister's detachment to mean that the United States was to be regarded simply as another foreign country, different from any other only by reason of its power, not because of any "special relationship" such as other prime ministers had striven to attain. In the days immediately before their exit from Vietnam in 1975, if the United States was special it was because of its proximity and its strength, not because of any allegedly shared ideals.

This was by no means the unanimous view in the Department, but those who disagreed seldom found reason for saying so. The dividing line would have been between those whose work gave them a primarily economic view of things as compared with those who dealt mostly with the other political factors. Vietnam was going badly for the Americans at home as well as on the battlefield. Draft dodgers were arriving in Canada declaring that the very air was different. Black Americans were in something close to open revolt. As compared to Americans, Canadians were feeling pretty good about themselves and trying, not very hard, to keep from smirking.

Viewed in retrospect, there was probably no need for most of the excitement the Third Option paper produced. It later became evident that the main object of the exercise was to produce a paper on relations with the United States that would fill a blank in the grand design of *Foreign Policy for Canadians,* and that objective was achieved with its publication. Certainly there was very little follow-through. The same lack of continuing prime ministerial interest in policy decisions once they were made has been alleged in respect of China. In that case, it must be recognized that the expectations were too high and when they were not met, the business community's interest in China declined. Nevertheless, again in retrospect, the early ventures of the Trudeau government into foreign affairs were enthusiastically pursued through the conceptual stages but were left to their own fate when it came to implementation.

Within the Department *Foreign Policy for Canadians* had been represented as standing instructions to the relevant divisions operating in their respective areas. As noted earlier, with some exceptions the booklets were pretty much codifications of existing policies and their influence on the work in the Department was not of great significance. This is not to belittle their importance because, as public documents, they had informed Canadians as never before on what the country's foreign operations were all about. Nevertheless they gave rise to some ridiculous ideas. Experts from something called the Bureau of Methods and Management came to the Department to see how it was implementing the instructions contained in the relevant booklets and find out if anyone was straying too far from the objectives set during the budgetary process. Their assumption was that day-to-day decisions were being made by reference to some objective contained in *Foreign Policy for Canadians*. The attitude of the visiting expert was that of an architect visiting a construction site to see if the contractor was putting the right amount of sand in the concrete. Although this didn't last very long and had little effect, it did produce some cynicism about "methodology."

The real importance of the new method of operating was the involvement in the budgetary process of the other departments with operational programmes abroad. Trade and Commerce, Immigration, the Canadian International Development Agency (CIDA), Finance and occasionally the RCMP, Health and Welfare, and Public Works took part in deciding priorities among missions abroad and within them. External still ran only three substantive programmes of its own, information abroad, consular services and the Passport Office. It was fighting hard to maintain a position in respect of foreign operations comparable to that of a central government agency, with the right to have the last word on any matter affecting Canada's position abroad. But there can be no doubt that management by objectives was the beginning of the erosion of the Department's undisputed primacy in matters of foreign policy.

The practice of diplomacy is regularly haunted by its own tendency to present itself as an arcane mystery that lesser mortals can't be expected to understand. Politicians, whose own art involves acquiring instant expertise, are particularly reluctant to accept the diplomat as having any real professional status. This is a recurrent theme in the way all governments deal with their foreign ministries, but it is especially relevant to the way in which the Canadian government of the seventies dealt with the Department of External Affairs.

It was particularly hard for those around the Prime Minister who had not worked in the field to understand how little of its own foreign agenda a sovereign state in the geopolitical position of Canada could actually control. Most of a foreign ministry's time and energy is spent simply reacting to unsolicited and unanticipated business forced on it by the outside world and in servicing the system itself, moving basic information around the world and keeping the home base and missions abroad in good operating condition. The process seems wasteful and inefficient until it is suddenly needed. The protection and advancement of national interests is more often a matter of trying to prevent bad things from happening than it is of making good things happen. This sort of talk was regarded as a form of special pleading, but the idea that the foreign ministry of a Middle Power could operate on the basis of a preconceived agenda, even that it could spend the greater part of its time and energy in dealing with matters of its own choice, was nonsense. Even superpowers spend as much energy reacting to events beyond their control as they do trying to have their way in the world if, indeed, the two can be separated.

None of this precludes having objectives. Quite the reverse; it requires particularly clear objectives. The best diplomatic practitioners (as distinct from megalomaniacs) do not pursue objectives according to a timetable. They have their objectives in mind all of the time, no matter what subject is being addressed. By exercising ingenuity they work their own aspirations into other people's agendas. In the early seventies the Japanese Foreign Ministry (Gaimusho), for instance, had no economic department; economic considerations were a part of all aspects of its foreign operations. Territorial security is not just a matter of having soldiers, aircraft and ships in the right place at the right time; it can also be affected by the terms on which a country sells fish. A first-class foreign ministry must be in a position to see all the interrelationships in the context of national objectives and interests and draw the necessary conclusions to its government's attention.

To someone working in the Department, particularly in the early Trudeau years, methodology sometimes seemed more important than substance — the medium driving the message. The nature of the Department's business made it a poor candidate for this sort of treatment. *Ad hoc*-ery, although frowned upon and disavowed, continued to flourish, to be justified when necessary after the event by reference to some budgetary objective. But the linkage between making a budget and running a foreign ministry remained tenuous. The Department could budget to open a new embassy in Asia as a matter of priority but when the balloon went up in the Middle East, that was where the money went and, usually, not at the Department's insistence but because of the government's desire to respond to public pressures that no budget could have anticipated.

About 1974, "Operation Delphi" took place. It was an opinion survey conducted by a behaviourist political science professor retained by the Department. Its purpose was to find out what the External staff, regardless of their job, thought about our relations with the United States. The opinion of the rankest neophyte working on French Equatorial Africa was given the same weight as that of people who had worked on US affairs for years. Moreover, the survey insisted on anonymity, apparently based on the assumption that public servants were too gutless to say what they thought for fear of offending someone higher up in the hierarchy. In fact, the opinions garnered by "Delphi" were pretty conventional and no more was heard of them, but the fact that an attempt was made to measure and quantify policies in such a sensitive and complex area in this manner says something about the atmosphere of the time.

These were the years when much energy was put into flow charts, critical paths, responsibility diagrams (tree charts were passé) and the analysis of decision-making processes. It was an enjoyable game and members of the Department entered into the spirit of it with things like a "wiring diagram" purporting to show the flow of information and decision-making authority throughout the Department. Unfortunately, it showed no place for the busiest junction box of them all, the departmental cafeteria where information moved swiftly and along lines that would defy definition.

Mr Trudeau's age of reasons was a heady time. Anything could be questioned, all options were open and no proposition was likely to be dismissed out of hand. It was also disturbing for the managers of the Department to be forever trying to anticipate and ward off those who wanted "to pull things up by the roots to see how they were growing," as a British Royal Commissioner once described what so often happened to the Foreign Office in his country.

Thus, under management by objectives, budgets were to be constructed by assessing the relative importance of each post or operating programme to the advancement of some objective mentioned in *Foreign Policy for Canadians*. Resources in money and manpower would then be assigned as needed to do the job. From the purely administrative point of view the new process was in all honesty a great improvement on the ways in which the Department had traditionally run itself. For the most part, the new approach served well at budget time in rationalizing the process of arriving at new balancing acts, although it could not always justify the conclusions that were reached. There were too many things that had to be done whether they had any relevance to The Book or not. There were also too many conflicting demands on the resources available that had to be negotiated with all the parties concerned. But the real downside was that External had pretty well lost its power to control the country's foreign operations.

The Department's administration had always been a barely controlled débâcle, ever threatening to collapse but never actually doing so. As already noted, anyone who could be persuaded to take on its administration was given a free hand, up to the point where the decision might affect a matter of foreign policy. At that point the hierarchy would intervene and the administrator would be left to clean up the mess. This system came to an end under the new regime when, for the first time, the Department acquired the services of a high-grade professional administrator in the person of Larry O'Toole who, amid much wailing and gnashing of teeth, succeeded in linking policy decisions to the administrative decisions that they implied. Thanks to him and prodded by the Treasury Board, management by objectives was made to make some sense. It was not done by following a master blueprint but by the very laborious process of bringing together all the parties concerned, putting the bag of money on the table and haggling over whether the new body going to Islamabad should be from External, Trade and Commerce or CIDA. Once the process (which bore a passing resemblance to the "floating crap game" of a bygone era) was completed, the result became less of a blueprint than a wish list that left enough flexibility (in the form of an undersecretarial slush fund) to deal with the unexpected.

Larry, an outsider from the Treasury Board, and Bill Lockhart, the military signaller who some years earlier had revolutionized the Department's communications, between them kept External Affairs in business at a time when the Prime Minister himself was said to have wondered if Canada really needed a foreign ministry at all. Perhaps, the argument went, the things External did could be done better by the departments responsible for the same programmes within Canada, with maybe a little help from the PMO. These ideas would have carried more weight had it not been for the Department's control of an efficient worldwide communications network and a long-overdue ability to administer itself.

So from a general euphoria over the arrival of Pierre Trudeau as Prime Minister, it wasn't long before there was a good deal of tension within External. There had been the perceived snub of appointing Ivan Head as foreign policy advisor; the review of foreign policy that produced *Foreign Policy for Canadians*, which seemed to be a challenge to the sacred cows in External's pasture; and finally, the Department's budgets in which every department with operations abroad had a say. The most sensitive souls in External were both sorry for themselves and puzzled. Why would someone as obviously intelligent and perceptive as Pierre Trudeau not have seen External and its denizens as his natural allies in Ottawa? After all, he was really one of them. Wasn't he?

There were several "explanations" for the PM's coolness toward the Department. One version had it that Trudeau had written the External exams but, for some reason, had not been invited in. The Public Service Commission goes to extraordinary lengths to protect this sort of information and it is unlikely that, supposing this had actually occurred, anyone with access to the information would have let it out. The story did circulate, however, but always as a doubtful tale. It is hard to imagine the young Trudeau hankering after a career in External or, if offered one, taking it — or, if he'd been refused, giving a damn.

There was another myth about Trudeau's lack of enchantment with External — an incident said to have taken place in Yugoslavia where a wandering young man in scruffy clothes came to the Canadian Embassy in Belgrade late one Friday, having lost his money and his passport. Whoever dealt with him was said to have refused to do anything until Monday morning and the future Prime Minister was obliged to spend a cold and hungry weekend (some versions said in a jail cell) presumably thinking about what he would do to External Affairs when he became Prime Minister.

There is, of course, no need to find personal reasons for Trudeau's attitude toward External. There were individuals and institutions about town who held no brief for External Affairs and no doubt some of the inherited glamour was wearing thin. Although External still had perhaps the most highly qualified aggregation of public servants in Ottawa and though the Department did what was expected of it pretty effectively, and although the people at the top of the Department were hyper-conscious of how other public servants felt about it, many of its people were seen to take themselves far too seriously. It may be sufficient to recall the difficulties the Department had in taking up some of the challenges presented by the new Prime Minister and its difficulty in coming to terms with the new people he brought with him. Indeed, the Department soon realized that things were going to be different and it did move to meet the managerial challenge in particular, but not before some prejudices had consolidated into a determination to cut it down to size. More than likely there was nothing the Department could have done that would have saved its traditional position as the country's principal diplomatic instrument.

The new approach very soon made itself felt at the heart of External — its personnel management. As part of the rationalization process managerial experts determined that there were only five identifiable and distinct jobs in the Foreign Service career stream. Up until then the Department and Trade and Commerce had had Foreign Service Officers grades 1 through 10, the topmost being occupied by a handful of their most important operators. The word "Officer" was also dropped from the title of the category and the top jobs in all departments, including External, were to share a common category called "Executive." The reason behind this appears to have been one that the Department itself had espoused: the generalist argument that a bright, well-educated, briefable person could be trained to do anything. This was carried to the point, however, where management was the name of the game and what was to be managed was of secondary importance. A senior person, it seemed, could be moved from Fisheries to Health and Welfare without any change of designation and do as good a job as if he had gone through all the career stages in the same department. The idea of making a career by becoming an expert in your field was replaced by the idea of becoming of an expert in managing departmental resources, in the same way that top management in business regularly moved without difficulty from one branch of industry to another. Managers were what was wanted; other expertise could be bought cheaply.

Once management became an objective in government, the rest followed. If External Affairs was no longer considered to be a repository of any special wisdom, the Department did not need the great numbers of the bright and the briefable that were labouring there in relatively subordinate positions. The PM's interest in revising the process of government produced a great need for intelligent, broken-in public servants to implement the changes. Where better to find them than in External? Not that the hunt was confined to it.

The Public Service Commission in the early seventies had established something called "Data Stream," a computer-based system of collating information on members of the public service. The forms asked several pages of questions about qualifications and interests that invited the filler-in to make a pitch for advancement, if not in his present job then by going elsewhere in the public service. Not everybody in the Department was interested in working elsewhere. Some did not seem to have given the possibility of advancement in another department very much attention and neglected to fill in the Data Stream form. Failure to respond brought a terse "It is noted that you have declined to provide the information necessary to complete your record. Please note that you cannot be identified in a search." There were recidivist members of the Foreign Service who liked what they were doing and had no desire to be "identified in a search." Data Stream, however, never gave up and the government did have its way, drawing off some of the best members of the Foreign Service into other parts of the public service. No doubt the general level of the public service was improved but External was weakened at its most vulnerable point — the commitment and experience of its personnel.

There had always been some movement between the Department and the Privy Council Office (PCO) or to temporary duty in the PMO, where the link of the individual with External was often maintained. The new migrations were quite different. In the early Trudeau years there was a steady exodus of middle-grade Foreign

Service personnel who went to jobs higher up in the public service hierarchy but with no obvious connection to their former jobs and who had little or no intention of returning to them. Allan Gotlieb, who had joined the Department in 1957, went to become Deputy Minister of Communications in 1968. After some years occupied primarily with domestic issues, he returned to External as Undersecretary. David Kirkwood after nineteen years with External moved to the Privy Council Office and went on to National Defence. Peter Roberts became the Prime Minister's press officer and went from there to a new career in the cultural field. He returned to External, where he paid his dues as Ambassador to Rumania before becoming Ambassador to the USSR and after that director of the Canada Council. Basil Robinson after twenty-five years in the Department was made Deputy Minister of Indian Affairs and Northern Development, returning to become Undersecretary in 1974 before going on to other things five years later. Blair Seaborn, who had joined External in 1948, left in 1970 to become Assistant Deputy Minister of Consumer and Corporate Affairs and on to higher things. John Starnes was appointed Director General of the RCMP Special Branch in 1970, where he stayed until retirement. Max Yalden after seventeen years in the Foreign Service became Deputy Minister of Communications and later returned to the Department between other appointments, including Commissioner of Official Languages and later of Human Rights. There were many others lost to the Department in their mid-career years. No doubt their service to the country was great in their other roles, but the Department paid the price.

By 1974, under Trudeau, the Department's preoccupation with administration and the budgetary process was taking priority over its now altered role in the management of the government's foreign policy. The idea of a profession of diplomacy, like the idea of a career within any single department, was no more. In the change the Department lost the services of some of its brightest people at a time when the Department, the country, and quite possibly the Prime Minister himself needed dedicated professionals to conduct Canada's increasingly complicated international business. Among the more pressing demands was the problem that one of the Department's most distinguished *emeriti,* John Holmes, president of the Canadian Institute of International Affairs, called "Living with Uncle."

7

Sharp Impressions

Mitchell Sharp became Secretary of State for External Affairs under Pierre Trudeau in 1968. He was well known in the Department, first as a public servant and later as a minister, first of Trade and Commerce and then of Finance, under Pearson. As a public servant, Sharp had worked his way to the top and then had gone into private life to establish himself as a businessman, heading one of Canada's biggest international enterprises. However, as Foreign Minister he was an unknown quantity.

Any initial reservations quickly faded. Mitchell Sharp soon became known as someone who thoroughly understood the relationship between public servant and politician and knew how to get the most out of the people who worked for him. In the course of the six years he served as minister, this became the basis of great mutual respect.

Every Secretary of State for External Affairs has to come to terms with the fact that prime ministers can and will intervene in areas that they find of particular interest. Under Pierre Trudeau this came to mean that the Prime Minister's Office would manage those aspects of foreign policy that interested the PM. At the outset that promised to be a very long list, but as time went on, the Prime Minister's international interests diminished, leaving Mitchell Sharp and his Department free to conduct the country's foreign operations, in most areas, most of the time.

The first qualification of a good minister from the public servant's point of view is that he should carry weight in cabinet. The accepted departmental opinion of Trudeau in the early seventies was that he was a good listener, but that no one, with the possible exception of two or three personal friends who dated back to his Montreal days, exerted much influence on him. Sharp was not an exception to the rule, but he had been an early supporter of the PM and was at least a political friend. Although he could not be expected to sway the PM, nevertheless, for those who worked closely with him, he was very nearly a perfect Secretary of State for External Affairs and on several accounts.

First there was his background as an ex-public servant who knew how to motivate and inspire his officials. He also knew the Ottawa scene and how it worked better than most politicians and many public servants. Then, he was briefable and did his homework; he read papers written for him even if they were longer than two pages, the cynic's idea of the maximum ministerial attention span. Mitchell Sharp picked up points quickly and was often well ahead of his would-be briefer. There was nothing devious about him. He would argue issues and he would make decisions. But what commanded loyalty were his understanding of the Department and his skill in using it.

During the negotiation to recognize the People's Republic of China, the minister's interventions were crucial and based on transparent common sense. When, at the last minute, the Chinese said they wanted the joint statement of intent that was to form the basis of a press release to be formally signed, the departmental legal people objected that it had not been negotiated as an international accord and would have to be redrafted before it could be signed. When the matter came to the minister, he told the lawyers to relax. If the Chinese intended to keep the agreement, signing wouldn't hurt; if they didn't, then signing wouldn't help since no one was going to take them to court. The document got signed. Later on, during the second Vietnam entanglement and disentanglement, his direction was equally clear and constructive.

Sharp continued to take a great interest in China after relations had been established. When Chang Wen-chin, the third Chinese Ambassador in about two years, arrived in Ottawa in 1973, Sharp arranged a private dinner with half a dozen people, mostly from the Department, who were concerned with China. The new Ambassador had a number of special credentials, the most important of which was that he had been a close collaborator of Chou En-lai in ending the isolationism that had been a characteristic of the Cultural Revolution. Chang had put his name to a paper that later became public and drew the wrath of the hardliners. The story went that he had been sent off to Ottawa by Chou En-lai to keep him out of harm's way.

After dinner in front of the fireplace at 7 Rideau Gate, the government's hospitality centre, Sharp led off asking about the internal situation in China. Gradually the questions got more and more pointed and Chang's answers became more and more informative.

By the end of the evening, those present probably knew more than most Westerners of what was happening in China at that time, how the Cultural Revolution was being wound down and how people around the Chinese premier felt about China opening up to the outside world.

A few years later Chang was recalled for higher duties in Beijing and, as was his custom, Sharp gave the departing ambassador a lunch. The Canadian election campaign of 1974 was in full spate. The minister proposed the usual toasts to the health and prosperity of his Chinese guest and in return Chang proposed some of his own, including one to the health of the government of Canada and its success at the polls. The public servants present eyed each other but none moved a finger toward a glass. Mitchell took over. He'd drink to that gladly, he said, but his public service colleagues couldn't. With grace and humour he gave the Chinese present a quick seminar on the Canadian constitution and everyone drank to something else.

Mitchell Sharp's tenure of office was dominated by concerns for the American relationship. It began with the Chinese initiative on which Washington had to be kept informed without being given a veto. It continued with Sharp's publication of the Third Option paper, which was interpreted in Washington as a form of anti-Americanism, and it peaked, at least in terms of hours consumed, early in 1973 when Canada first became involved in (and then escaped from) the last Vietnam "armistice" supervision arrangement.

In January of 1973 negotiations in Paris, punctuated by bombings in Indochina, finally produced a piece of paper that all the belligerents in Vietnam could sign. By then Canada had had nineteen years' experience in Indochina. Well over a hundred members of the Department (and many more of the Canadian armed forces) had spent at least a year in North Vietnam, South Vietnam, Laos or Cambodia ("Chaos and Lambodia," as John Holmes used to call them). This experience was to become a model of how peacekeeping operations should not be done. Canada had a ringside seat for much of what was going on, but no influence. It was there that the book was written on what criteria should be met before the government should agree to take part in future peacekeeping operations.

Many Canadians thought the country's role in Indochina did it no credit. There were allegations that while ostensibly serving the cause of international peace, we were in fact acting as agents of the United States: carrying their messages and bringing back intelligence, blindly defending American interests within the International Commission for Supervision and Control (ICSC) and selling arms to a belligerent country contrary to our own arms export policies. There was enough truth in the allegations to make it difficult to issue a blanket denial. Where the accusations stuck, pleas of extenuating circumstances, although sometimes valid, carried less and less conviction as time went on.

At the root of the matter was a fact that could not be stated publicly. Canada's entanglement in Indochina had more to do with our relationship with the United States than it did with supervising a non-existent armistice. At the same time Canadians in Indochina did acquire their own expertise and opinions about the war and its probable outcome. Neither the opinions nor the actions of the Canadians involved always supported those of the United States.

In the sale of arms we had the choice of either not selling any to our Nato ally or of selling them without conditions attached to their ultimate use. The loss of the American market would have made our own arms production impossible to sustain. The government did what most Canadian governments would have done in the circumstances; it gave priority to its own defence arrangements over its conflicting obligations as a purely nominal peacekeeper, there being no peace to keep. More than that, at the outset Canadians had supported American involvement in Indochina. It would be hard for anyone to say when exactly that changed. More than likely, Canadian opinion tracked opinion in the United States itself.

The Geneva Accord of 1954 was signed by Britain, France, the United States, China and North and South Vietnam. It purported to provide a demarcation line between the two parts of Vietnam, establish arrangements for the movement of refugees and lay down conditions for an armistice. Canada, along with Poland and India, was co-opted without consultation to be a member of the International Commission for Supervision and Control. India was designated to chair the Commission. There were really three related bodies, one for Laos, one for Cambodia and one for Vietnam, the last being divided, with one group based in Saigon and one in Hanoi. In the very early days the ICSC served a useful function in helping refugees move across the Demilitarized Zone that separated North from South Vietnam. But in very short order it became paralysed. The fatal flaw in the Geneva Accord was that while the South Vietnamese and their allies saw the agreement as the basis of a permanent arrangement, the North saw it simply as a means of catching its breath before continuing its holy war for the extension of the philosophy and rule of Ho Chi Minh (and North Vietnam) to all of Indochina.

The Accord provided that although the sides in Indochina were allowed to replace worn or obsolete military equipment piece for piece, no additional items of equipment were to be brought into the area. It was the duty of the ICSC to monitor this provision. In the early sixties, this was the way the work of the Commission was described to Canadian visitors in Indochina:

> A team consisting of a Canadian, a Polish and an Indian military officer were at a railway station on the frontier between North Vietnam and China.
>
> "Look," the Canadian member would say to the Indian chairman, "there's a trainload of Soviet tanks rolling into Vietnam."
>
> The Indian chairman would then ask the Pole what he saw and the latter would reply that he could see no tanks.
>
> "Well," the Canadian would ask the Indian, "what do you see?"
>
> To this the Indian would reply, "I am a neutral chairman and unless you two can agree on what you see, I can see nothing."

A similar team operating at a South Vietnamese port where American tanks were coming ashore would have quite a different conversation. The Pole would see US tanks landing, the Canadian would agree that they were indeed US tanks and the Indian chairman would then report, by unanimous decision, that there had been a violation of the accord by the United States and South Vietnam.

Canadian delegations had the choice of either letting the Commission become an instrument of North Vietnamese policy or of becoming useless. The response was obvious and the Commission quickly became useless. Canadian attempts to wind up the Commission over the years were unsuccessful; none of the parties was willing to let this last vestige of the Geneva Accord disappear. In Ottawa, no one was happy with the role the country was playing, except to the extent that it provided a reason for resisting American pressure to send Canadian forces to fight alongside theirs. By the early seventies the Department had managed to wind down the ICSC to a heartbeat. Operations in Phnom Penh had been concluded entirely and External (at any rate) was looking forward to getting out altogether, once the Paris negotiation finally ended.

It was not to be. Washington informed the Department that the new arrangements being worked out in Paris in 1972–73 provided for a successor to ICSC to be called the International Commission for Control and Supervision (ICCS). More than the names were similar. The Department was allowed to see selected bits of the draft of the document then on the verge of being signed. The reaction of External's Indochina hands, by now sophisticated experts on any aspect of the subject, was instant depression. There were no believers. The United States intended to move out, the North Vietnamese had conceded next to nothing and what they had given was intended more to save face than to provide guarantees to the South Vietnamese. The truce-supervising arrangements looked very much like those of the Geneva Accord except that there would be four members — Canada, Hungary, Indonesia and India — and the chairmanship would rotate.

After many years of participation in a wide variety of truce supervisory arrangements, the Canadian military and the Department had developed some firm ideas. Their distilled wisdom on the subject had been passed on to the Secretary-General of the United Nations, among others. After looking at the proposed new Vietnamese arrangements and measuring them against the Canadian yardsticks, Mitchell Sharp told Washington where he thought there would be difficulties and where they should try to strengthen the provisions External had been allowed to see. By then the negotiation in Paris was in its final and toughest stage and there could be no question of reopening closed clauses, so what we saw was what we got.

The provisions External and National Defence thought essential if any peacekeeping operation was to succeed should have provided

- a clear and enforceable mandate;
- agreement among the parties to cease firing;
- agreement by all concerned that Canada should participate;
- arrangements for finding a basis for a long-term settlement;
- peacekeepers in sufficient number and of a kind suitable for the task in hand;
- a single identifiable authority to whom to report, preferably the Secretary-General of the United Nations; and
- adequate logistical and financial provisions.

In the Department's view the Paris Agreement did not meet these criteria in several crucial areas. It did not provide the basis of a long-term settlement and, most particularly, it did not provide for any independent party to which the Commission could report its findings. Like its predecessor, the ICCS could report only to the signatories — i.e., to those who were either the victims of a breach (who knew they had been victimized) or the violators (who knew they had been violating).

These objections were made known to all concerned but even as this was being done, it was realized that Canada would not be able to escape the logic of some of its own actions. Earlier in January 1973, the same month in which the truce agreement was signed, the Canadian House of Commons, in a rare public gesture of criticism of the United States, had passed a resolution deploring US bombing in Indochina. The Americans were now, it seemed, about to do what we had been urging and were getting out of the area. They wanted Canada to help them do this. How could we refuse?

In February, shortly after the agreement was signed, a delegation headed by Mitchell Sharp attended an international conference intended to discuss the post-hostilities period in Vietnam. They went with some aid money in hand and with the primary purpose of creating an overview group to whom the ICCS could report. They had no success. Their first preference, to report to the UN Secretary-General, had been rejected in advance by the signatories.

The people in the Department who had been involved with Indochina over the previous nineteen years saw the Paris document, *Restoring Peace in Vietnam*, as a means of disengaging US forces from this unwinnable war. They also had the vision of Canada in the new ICCS as a sort of American surrogate presence after the American forces had left. They were determined that if Canadians had to be involved in this new arrangement, the first concern was to make sure they weren't trapped. The Department's first line of defence was to advise the government to say "no"; the second was to accept for a minimum period, thirty days, to see how things were going and to see if our judgement of what would happen was right. This was done and a further sixty-day trial period followed. That committed Canada to stay on the job up to March 31, 1973, by which time the minister would make a further decision about remaining on.

Once it was agreed to send people out, or to rebaptize those who were still there as ICCS, there were decisions to make. Who should head the Canadian delegation and what instructions should be given him? The choice, once mentioned, was never debated. Michel Gauvin, then Ambassador in Greece, had a distinguished military record in World War II and had served not only in Indochina but also in the Congo during the UN peacekeeping operations there. He was known as a no-nonsense plainspoken sort of person who could hold his own with his colleagues-to-be in the ICCS. In support of Gauvin, Vernon Turner was prevailed upon to go as deputy commissioner and political cal advisor. Vern had also had Indochina experience as well as postings in Eastern Europe and in the United Nations. It was a very successful combination, illustrating the range of talent that was still available to the Department in the early seventies.

The Department was determined to provide the best expertise and the strongest leadership available for what was bound to be a difficult and sensitive job. It was important that Canada be seen doing its best to make the system work and yet not get inextricably involved. In drawing up instructions to the delegation, the Department tried to compensate for the absence of a third party to whom the Commission would report, which had been the source of much of the frustration in the old ICSC. It was decided to offset the absence of a reporting authority by what was called "the Open Mouth Policy."

Gauvin was told that after every meeting of the Commission he was to inform the media, or anyone interested, on what had gone on inside; not just what the Canadians had said but what everyone else had said as well. This, of course, is diplomatic heresy. One can report publicly one's own position and actions but it was for the others to report theirs. The delegation let it be known in advance that it intended to do this because there was no authority other than world opinion to whom the Commission could report and, after all, the world was very much interested in what was happening in Vietnam. Gauvin thoroughly enjoyed the role and did a superb job, at least judging by the reactions of the first chairman, a Hungarian who thought it very ill-mannered for a colleague to report publicly and in detail how he had obstructed a Commission investigation that could have embarrassed the North Vietnamese.

The Canadian armed forces weighed in with their usual efficient enthusiasm. Major-General D.A. McAlpine was named to be the chief military advisor. The Canadians were in their places when they had said they would be. There was, however, a contretemps about the channels of communication involving the higher levels in National Defence (DND). The Department insisted that this was primarily a diplomatic operation and that all communications should go through External's Communications Centre and be addressed to Gauvin, the Head of Delegation. The people in DND did not take kindly to being out of direct communication with their own forces and kept insisting that signals about "boots and laces" should not have to go through External. There were some compromises and also some evasions of External as a line of communications. The Department discovered by accident that a weekly situation report was being made by the military commander in Saigon to his superior in Ottawa by videotape that by-passed External, although it was sent through External's diplomatic bag service. The debate over communications continued until it was made irrelevant by Canada's withdrawal from the Commission.

By declaring Canada's participation for a trial period, the Department indicated that from Day One its main preoccupation had been to find a fail-safe system by which the decision, when it came, would not be whether to pull out of the ICCS but whether to stay in it. It was acknowledged that the agreement had to be given a chance to work in the way it had been presented to us — as "peace with honour" — but if it became clear, instead, that it was going to work the way the North Vietnamese had intended — a breathing space followed by the unification of the two Vietnams — Canada would not have to quit, we could just decline to renew our contract. Mitchell Sharp had put it very bluntly. Canada, he said, would "not take part in a charade."

With some possible exceptions in DND, it was generally accepted in Ottawa that this was the sensible and proper course to follow. There had been one briefing for the Prime Minister and some other select persons in the Operations Room of the East Block. The reactions were reassuring for all concerned. Ivan Head had ordered in some fast food, which was eaten while the briefing was under way. It was to become known in the press as the Colonel Sanders briefing.

Toward the end of the first ninety days, the end of March 1973, it was time to make a new commitment or get out. Sharp decided that he wanted to see something of what was going on and talk directly to the people on the scene before making his recommendation to cabinet. A dozen or so officials and media representatives accompanied the minister to Indochina. The group spent part of three days in Saigon, with a visit to the embattled Mekong Delta. Overnight in Vientiane, Laos, the minister met Prince Souvanna Phouma. He also spoke to the Ambassador of the United States, alleged to have been the only diplomat in the world who could call down a bomber strike. The minister left early the next day, stopped over in Hanoi for a prolonged lunch-discussion with the political heirs of Ho Chi Minh and continued on to Guam, Winnipeg and Ottawa. Crossing the International Dateline, the party arrived in Ottawa the same day it had left Laos.

In the Department there was one particular reason for wanting the minister and his group to talk with its people in Vietnam. There had been some disconcerting discrepancies between what the operators in the Department were hearing from Washington and what they were hearing from External's own people in the field in Vietnam. There was one view that whenever there was a conflict between its own and the American sources of information the Department should assume its own sources were accurate and that judgements should be made on that basis. Because this view was not unanimously held in Ottawa, it was important to find out from the Canadians on the spot what they thought about the conflicting reports.

Some suspicions were confirmed in a general way during the visit to the Mekong Delta, where fighting had resumed. The information coming from American sources was to the effect that, on the whole, the armistice was holding and such fighting as there was had involved only local communist forces. According to these sources, there was no evidence of any fresh infiltration down the Ho Chi Minh Trail from North Vietnam. The point was crucial for continued Canadian participation, since North Vietnamese involvement would mean that the truce was not holding, that North Vietnam did not intend to allow the Paris Agreement to lead to a long-term settlement, and that our continuing on the ICCS would, indeed, be a charade. Canadians on the spot, as well as some local South Vietnamese representatives the minister met, were satisfied that the local communists could not have mounted actions on the scale that had taken place without support from the North. Other evidence obtained through the interrogation of prisoners also pointed in the same direction. In any event, those who were with the minister were satisfied that the information coming from the Canadian sources was correct and that the armistice was not holding. Later events, of course, proved North Vietnamese intentions beyond argument.

On his return, the minister decided that Canada should commit itself to a further ninety days, making then six months in all, and that well before the end of June we should make up our minds about the long term. Some in the Department were depressed by the decision and imagined that we were getting sucked in to the point where we might never be able to get out. However, that was not the way it happened. By late May the government had decided not to renew our commitment. It informed Washington at the highest level that Canada would remain beyond June 30 but not later than July 31, to allow adequate time in which to find a successor. No detailed reasons were given for our decision, which we simply said was a result of our nineteen years' experience in Vietnam. All concerned were assured that our action was not to be taken as a criticism of the Paris Agreement itself.

During the six-month Canadians participation there were two incidents in Vietnam involving Canadians; one helped to make the decision not to stay while the other served to confirm the judgement. The first came in early April when a Canadian officer, Captain Laviolette, was killed in an ICCS helicopter shot down, it was believed, by North Vietnamese forces near Khe Sanh in South Vietnam. It occurred about the same time that the Department was advising its man in Saigon that since the government was considering leaving the Commission, there was no point in trying to pursue investigations that were being obstructed by the Hungarian member of the Commission. Captain Laviolette's death reinforced the belief that Canadian lives should not be jeopardized by trying to apply a truce that at least one of the parties clearly did not wish to keep.

At this point what seemed to be a DND argument came in from Saigon advocating an "activist" policy for as long as Canada remained on the Commission, using the fate of Captain Laviolette as a reason for greater rather than less activity. It is a military ideal not to withdraw under fire, but peacekeeping is not a conventional military operation. In peacekeeping it is axiomatic that if the parties concerned do not want peace, peace cannot be enforced.

The second incident was the kidnapping of two Canadian officers and two of their Vietnamese staff, which occurred after Canada had given notice of its intention to depart. It gave rise to the same sorts of arguments. Just a month before our time in Vietnam was to run out, two Canadian captains with two Vietnamese employees were taken by troops of the Provisional Revolutionary Government of South Vietnam. Although they had left their camp with the concurrence of the chairman of the team (still the Hungarian member), they were accused of improper activities, presumably spying on behalf of the United States. This was denied, but the main Canadian claim was that the persons concerned were entitled under the Paris Agreement to diplomatic immunity and must be returned forthwith along with their Vietnamese personnel.

This affair revealed some of the latent differences in the Department over the nature of Canada's commitment to the Commission. There were those who were not prepared to accept the Canadian officers back unless they were accompanied by their Vietnamese staff. At one stage, when it was feared the kidnapped Canadians were wounded, a proposal was made to exchange them for two other Canadian officers pending a settlement of the fate of the Vietnamese. The Department even considered leaving a Canadian negotiating team in the neighbourhood after Canada's withdrawal from the Commission. It also faced the prospect of having to advise the minister that the Canadian delegation should leave Vietnam on schedule regardless of the fate of the unfortunate Vietnamese staff members. In the end none of these contingency plans had to be used; all four of the abducted persons were returned unharmed. If the government's resolve was being tested, it had passed with good marks.

Like everything to do with Canada's Vietnam ventures, arrangements for the Canadians' departure went down to the wire. Michel Gauvin, who was anxious to get back to his post in Athens, was to have left Vietnam earlier but had been asked to stay on until the missing captains were returned. As late as a week before the delegation was to depart, Washington was still unable to say who would be replacing Canada. (It turned out to be Iran.) The Canadians agreed to leave behind a small hand-over party but as the deadline approached, Vern Turner, who was in charge at the end, was told he should leave by July 31 or at the latest, August 1, which he did.

In anticipation of Canada's departure from the ICCS, the Department had set up an embassy under the absentee headship of Gordon Riddell, then our Ambassador in Bangkok. The post had three main functions: to be an expression of continuing Canadian interest in the fate of Vietnam after our departure from the Commission; to manage the aid programme to which we had committed ourselves after the Paris Agreement; and to look after consular and immigration affairs. Ed Scrabec was named chargé d'affaires in Saigon. He was a competent and tough-minded middle-grade FSO and he stayed in Saigon until the final débâcle in the spring of 1975. Even then Vietnam did not let the Canadians go easily. When the last External people were at the airport, about to depart, the chargé's Vietnamese driver tried to board the Canadian aircraft sent to take our people out. He had to be persuaded that his proper place was in Vietnam with his wife and children. The scene was witnessed by some members of the press who reported on the hard-heartedness of the Canadians involved.

Nothing could better illustrate the limitations that apply to a country's ability to set its own agenda in the field of international affairs than the history of Canada's more than twenty years' involvement in Vietnam. In 1954, when Canada had fewer than forty diplomatic missions in the entire world, few places could have had lower priority than Saigon, Hanoi, Vientiane and Phnom Penh. Without any consultation, the Powers at the Geneva Conference on Indochina, which included all the permanent members of the UN Security Council, signed an accord that put those places at the head of the list. In theory, Canada could have refused to take part, but it would have been irresponsible, forcing a delay in implementation that could have cost hundreds of lives. And there would have been a political price to be paid in terms of future bilateral relations with the signatories.

Between July of 1954 and April of 1975 more FSOs had developed expertise in Southeast Asia than, for instance, in Latin America, although Canada's national interests were quite the other way around. Hundreds of Canadian military personnel spent a year and more in Indochina. Two FSOs and perhaps a half dozen members of the armed forces died on service there and the Canadian taxpayer footed a substantial bill purely and simply as a payment on our dues as a member of the international community.

The establishment of relations with Beijing and the final extraction of Canada from its Indochinese involvement were among the most significant activities to which the Department gave its attention under Mitchell Sharp's direction. But there were others, notably the care and nourishment of the American connection. For instance, there was the episode of August 1971 known as the Nixon Shocks, a series of economic measures that drastically affected Canadian trade and showed again how vulnerable Canadian business was to decisions made in the USA. There was also the OPEC-inspired oil crisis of January 1974 when Canada was asked by Washington to pool its growing energy resources with America's diminishing ones.

The personality of the Prime Minister became an element in the bilateral relationship. As noted earlier, Trudeau's cool, rational approach to politics and his willingness to look at all options, even military neutrality, made Washington uneasy. His lively nonconformity was not understood and, for his part, he did not respond well to being crossed. It is possible that, like most of Trudeau's own

Canadian colleagues and opponents, American public figures were wary of having a public disagreement with him because they couldn't be sure how they'd look after the encounter.

On the other hand "Mitchell" (Sharp) and "Bill" (Rogers), the US Secretary of State, hit it off very well. They settled some of the outstanding issues relating to our reluctant peacekeeping activity in Vietnam directly and personally. Although the Prime Minister played his full part in dealing with Washington, both directly and through Ivan Head and Ivan's White House contacts (notably Henry Kissinger and Brent Scowcroft), the Secretary of State for External Affairs continued to be the channel of communications for most operational purposes.

There were some exceptions. Canadian Ambassadors to Washington had always complained of being by-passed by other departments in Ottawa. There was one occasion during Marcel Cadieux's tour as Ambassador in Washington between 1970 and 1975 when an executive assistant of the then Minister of National Defence flew in from Ottawa by ministerial aircraft to spend a day in the office of Senator Edward Kennedy. Although it was during the Republican era of Richard Nixon, nobody had thought to ask the Ambassador in Washington if it would be a good idea for a Canadian cabinet minister's assistant to be in open contact with the most prominent Democratic senator in Washington. This sort of thing infuriated Marcel, who was once heard to explode: " I don't run an embassy here. I run a pissoir and a hot dog stand and no one comes near me unless they want to use one or the other."

Occasionally these casual contacts between Ottawa and Washington would present External with a *fait accompli* on some issue being negotiated. An agreement was once reached on the telephone between the Canadian Minister of Agriculture and his American opposite number about the movement of beef across the border. The Department, with Mitchell Sharp's blessing, tried to put some restraints on these contacts in the hope that it would at least be kept informed of them. The attempt was viewed with alarm by one minister in particular who made it very clear that, as he put it, he did not intend to get External's permission every time he wanted to talk to his American colleague on the phone. The only consolation for the Department was that the US State Department probably wasn't any better informed of these exchanges than External was. Nonetheless, the potential for driving wedges between competing interests within the other country was enormous.

The person who, with Mitchell Sharp, kept the Department functioning effectively during the trials of the early Trudeau years was Ed Ritchie, who had swapped jobs with Cadieux and become Undersecretary, the operating head of the Department, from 1970 until that day in September of 1974 when he drove himself, literally and figuratively, to the intensive care unit of an Ottawa hospital. Comparisons are invidious, but it would be surprising if any of the succeeding undersecretaries would disagree that he was the last of the breed of what Granatstein called "Men of Influence": persons who had appeared during the war and had contributed so much to the reputation of the Canadian public service generally and the Department in particular. They were not so much giants among lesser mortals as they were unselfish people with an intense sense of duty and some very clear ideas about the nature and destiny of their country. Ritchie did not return to the Undersecretary's Office on the eighth floor of the Pearsoneum and the stresses there that had undermined his health.

It had been Ed Ritchie's idea that the residents of Killers' Row, the assistant undersecretaries (AUSSEAs), should be taken out of the direct line of responsibility between himself and those who managed the Department's day-to-day operations. Instead of having to report through an AUSSEA, just about anyone with an operational responsibility was given direct access to the Undersecretary himself. This imposed an enormous additional burden on Ritchie. AUSSEAs became advisors to the Undersecretary on the one hand and to the Heads of Division on the other. The effect was that although the inhabitants of Killers' Row didn't exactly have their knives taken away, they were certainly blunted.

The system worked well, inasmuch as the Undersecretary had his finger on the Department's pulse and was better able to pass its advice to the minister and see that the government's wishes were known at the working level. On the other hand it increased the burden on the Undersecretary. The Department had always been hard on its undersecretaries but it was hardest on Ed Ritchie.

The focus for most of the changes that took place in the management of the country's foreign affairs during Mitchell Sharp's ministry was something called the Interdepartmental Committee on External Relations (ICER), which had two *raisons d'être*. The first was to ensure full consultation among the departments operating abroad. The second was to examine the possibility of a reorganization that would unify all the principal agencies operating abroad.

Mitchell Sharp's time at the helm of External began with the Chinese initiative and ended soon after overseeing Canada's escape from the fiasco of Vietnam. After twenty years of frustration in Indochina, the Department, along with the Department of National Defence, had learned — or should have learned — that it was much easier to get into such operations than it was to get out of them.

During the summer of 1974 Allan MacEachen replaced Mitchell Sharp in the minister's office and, after Ed Ritchie's illness, John Halstead became Acting Undersecretary. At the time Halstead was also heavily involved in negotiating the "Contractual Link" with the European Economic Community (EEC). For nearly three months the Prime Minister deferred appointing a new Undersecretary; when Halstead raised the matter with the PMO there seemed to be some surprise that anyone was in any hurry.

The operating styles of Mitchell Sharp and Allan MacEachen were remarkably different and called for some adjustment. Sharp was highly organized and totally involved in the running of his Department. MacEachen was a political artist, less wedded to a routine while involved in everything of importance going on in Ottawa. As a result he required more from his officials.

In December, Basil Robinson, who had been extracted from the Department some years before, was appointed Undersecretary to general rejoicing in the Department but to the particular relief of those who had been holding the fort on the eighth floor of the Pearsoneum. Robinson had been Deputy Minister of Indian Affairs and Northern Development for the previous four years and was the first person to come back to run the Department after such a long absence from the field of diplomacy. This was the way the managerial revolution was supposed to work and it marked another phase in the Department's transition from an élite within the public service to a department of government like any other. The fact that Basil Robinson was one of the Department's own made the move not just possible but welcome.

8

Spies and Soldiers

The Canadian involvement in Vietnam and its disentanglement from it in 1973 illustrated how closely the Department was obliged to work with National Defence, although that episode was not typical of the sort of collaboration that went on from day to day. In terms of volume, most of the business conducted between the two organizations dealt with preparing for Nato ministerial meetings, disarmament, the non-proliferation of atomic weapons, status of forces agreements for the Canadian military stationed abroad, the export of military equipment and, of course, intelligence. All were areas that involved our relations with other countries and with international agencies. Although the two departments were the principal consumers of intelligence within the government, the Canadian intelligence community had a life of its own that should be taken up before returning to the discussion of other aspects of the Department's relations with the military.

Nothing in this account contains information that has not been published elsewhere. The point in going over it here is to try to give some idea of the part played by intelligence between 1950 and 1980 from the point of view of the user rather than the producer of intelligence.

Canadian intelligence operations, long a well-kept secret, were still not much in the public domain during the prime ministership of Pierre Trudeau. Since World War II when Canada got into the business on a large scale, hundreds of people had been sworn never to reveal things that were later to become common knowledge. As late as the early seventies the very term *sigint* (signals intelligence or the interception of communications) was never uttered in the presence of the unindoctrinated. Those with real first-hand knowledge of the business continued to be reluctant to talk, while in spite of later revelations, those who had to depend on the bits and pieces that had been published, extensive as they were, found it hard to put all the information available into a framework that made sense.

The rule of "need to know" ensured that very, very few people were in a position to see the whole picture, even though Canada's membership in an international intelligence community influenced both our foreign policies and the diplomacy used to implement them. At the same time, what we brought to the intelligence community, and the very fact that we were a part of it, was itself a foreign policy consideration, another Canadian interest in the international environment that had to be managed.

"Intelligence" is one of those words that means whatever the user wishes it to. At one end of the spectrum it is the same as "information" or even "data." At the other end it could mean something that had little or nothing to do with information. What might be called "executive" intelligence — dirty tricks, the "007" of fiction — dealt with direct but deniable intervention in the internal affairs of other countries. The most dramatic of this sort of activity would be assassination. There were many ways in which "intelligence," agencies could influence events in other countries: the suborning of foreign officials to do what you wanted; the use of "agents of influence" to put a favourable "spin" on policy matters; and direct sabotage — of a country's scientific or economic installations, for instance. Although there were some lapses from grace by the Special Branch of the RCMP in its domestic operations, no Canadian apparatus was authorized to try to manipulate the legitimate operations of other governments. Canadian interest was confined to the possibility of others using "dirty tricks" on us and the need to defend against them; in theory, Canadian intelligence was to be entirely defensive.

This created some problems. Gathering protected information from another country would be "offensive," while the other side of the same coin, the protection of information, "security" or "counter-intelligence," was essentially "defensive." Both, however, involved getting information about the other side. Although the motives may seem quite unrelated, what separated the two forms of intelligence was more of a distinction than a difference. When a defensive security operation attempted to penetrate the other side's apparatus to protect its own information the distinction became blurred. If a defensive operation, say an attempt to eavesdrop on a Soviet diplomat believed to be engaged in espionage against us, came up with information that had an offensive value over and above the security information being sought, how could the two be separated? What should one do with the offensive information that came our way? What if a security-based operation picked up a conversation about the other side's bargaining position on a commercial contract under negotiation? It would be hard to imagine that a government would refuse to use such information on the grounds that it only conducted defensive intelligence operations.

In spite of the difficulties in making the distinction, Canadian governments took the view that Canada's intelligence operations were defensive in intent. We would not send covert agents into foreign countries to pick up information for use in our bilateral dealings. Apart from liaison with foreign agencies and looking after the security of our embassies and delegations abroad, our security-intelligence operations would be conducted entirely within our own territory or, if outside Canada, with the knowledge and co-operation of the country concerned. At the same time, by reason of our membership in an international intelligence community, we did provide information about third parties acquired within Canada to other countries with which we had working arrangements; in return, we would receive intelligence from those same countries, at least some of which were very much engaged in offensive intelligence. These by-products of our security or counterintelligence operations that were of political or other interest were brought to the attention of those deemed to have a need to know, including, obviously, the political leadership.

For security reasons (and possibly because of some interdepartmental politics) a number of compartmentalized intelligence networks were established. The ideal was that the right hand should operate without knowing what the left hand was doing, except at certain specified points of contact. There had to be people who were tied into several of these nets and who could make their own cross-references. Otherwise, people working in the same areas would be working on the basis of different information with chaotic results.

At one time most of the intelligence threads went through the Department's hands and were managed both as an element in the country's foreign relationships and as sources of information on matters of international interest. Many of the networks were international in their scope and the raw intelligence collected by the participating states was made available to the other member states best equipped to process it. The refined intelligence product was then circulated to all members according to their expressed interests. However, national agencies also ran networks that permitted items to be seen only by their own nationals. If, for instance, an Australian agency happened upon some information about an American activity in the South Pacific of particular interest to Australia, it would be marked "Australian Eyes Only" and it would not go into the general budget of information available to all the other member states. On the other hand, the Australians might want the information to be seen, say, in London, and it might be sent on to the British net marked "Australian and British Eyes Only."

There was a convention that members of an intelligence network did not deliberately spy on each other on the grounds that to do otherwise would undermine the whole process. But diplomats generally and intelligence operators in particular were string-savers who couldn't possibly throw away any information about anyone that came to hand. If there were any operations mounted in violation of the convention they would have to have been exceptionally well protected. In any event all foreign ministries and security agencies protected their information from their allies just as zealously as from anyone else. The exchange of information about third parties was one thing; exchanges within the group about other members of the group was more delicate.

In the Department, intelligence reports were always very popular reading by those entitled to see them. They imparted a feeling of special status and they also created a strong sort of loyalty to the intelligence system by which insiders accepted responsibility for seeing that outsiders learned nothing about them. Intelligence reports were often titillating, sometimes amazing and usually interesting. It was a unique sensation to read an intelligence report of how one's conversation with a foreign diplomat has been reported by him to his capital, but apart from teaching people to be careful of how they spoke to foreign diplomats, the practical value of the information was not as great as it might seem to be at first blush.

It has been said that the Soviet government never believed anything it heard about a foreign country unless it received the information from a covert source. The Soviets pretended to believe that the statistics published by Western governments were cleverly falsified, either to deceive the KGB or their own people or both. Even though they were heavy subscribers to government publications, the chances were that they also were taken in by their own propaganda line. Their known preference for covert information set them up for deception by having misleading information passed to known agents in the hope that they might act on it.

Even for those less addicted to covert information than the Russians, there were fundamental problems in relying on information obtained entirely through intelligence operations. It was frequently not possible to act directly or openly on intelligence information without thereby letting the other side know that its security had been penetrated. Consequently, covertly obtained information could not be used to defend, say in Parliament, a course of action that was based on it. Moreover, the information itself could not, as a rule, be independently verified, and those who made political decisions based on covert intelligence ran the risk of being victimized by planted misinformation.

There was a further objection which applied to intelligence received from or through foreign agencies. In furtherance of some important policy objective, covert information that was passed on could be tilted or judiciously selected to produce a desired impression. Although experts say that raw intelligence is difficult to concoct, it has been done. The Gulf of Tonkin incident of 1964 in which intelligence was at best doctored, or at worst created, led to President Johnson getting enhanced presidential powers enabling him to wage war without declaring it in the manner prescribed by the US constitution. This same dubious information also led Prime Minster Pearson into giving his approval to the US bombing of Haiphong harbour.

Obviously, no intelligence source can doctor its information to delude its clients very often before the law of diminishing returns sets in. Judiciously used, however, selected and directed information did influence important decisions at critical moments. Over the longer term the selection of information that supports a favoured point of view and the down-playing of information that might conflict with it can gently turn a line of thinking from one direction toward a quite different one. This can be virtually undetectable but, considering that intelligence operations are the epitome of the amoral, any country receiving covert information from another country would be entitled to question the motives of those who were providing it. Indeed, it would be foolish not to operate on the assumption that a foreign source would be less inclined to provide intelligence that might damage its own interests and more inclined to forward information that supported its own national point of view. Clearly, enough inconvenient information would have to be passed along to maintain credibility in the system. The point is that in the intelligence market the rule "buyer beware" applies with full effect. Not just the original source of the information needs to be evaluated but the motives of those who passed it along.

This did not mean that information passed along by a friendly government would be totally discounted. Even selected information can be useful. For many years, the British government supplied Commonwealth countries with "Foreign Office Prints," excellent analytical reports from British diplomatic missions as well as background papers on a variety of international issues. No one ever suggested that those papers were prepared specially for the Commonwealth market. The British themselves could justify passing them along on the assumption that people who operated on the basis of the same information might well come to similar conclusions. Exchanges of information among diplomats served the same purpose. If other countries could be persuaded that your way of looking at a problem was sensible, persuading them to act on that basis would be simpler. The insidious thing about intelligence, however, was that it seemed to put the reader inside the head of the other side but because it precluded knowledge of how the information was obtained, much less a cross-examination of the source, the user very often could not be quite sure whether he was dealing with mere possibilities or real intentions, one person's opinion or a government's policy.

One thing that could be said about covert intelligence without reservation was that it alerted the recipient to possibilities for which confirmation could be sought elsewhere. There have been tragic failures to use intelligence intelligently, for instance the Pearl Harbor intercepts, which were never acted upon. In terms of Canada, a Middle Power with no world power ambitions, one could wonder whether the substantial price we paid in playing the game was worth what we got. On the other hand, as with small-town tea parties, it might have been unwise not to have been there if only to reduce the chances of becoming a target.

Those who have a vital piece of intelligence will make it available to those who don't have it when the issue is important enough. That was what the British did with an intercepted German telegram during World War I. A telegram from the German Foreign Minister to the German Embassy in Mexico was intercepted and deciphered by British Admiralty intelligence. It contained a wild idea for bringing Mexico into war against the United States. The British passed the information to the Americans who then had to weigh its contents against the motives of the British in providing it — obviously to foster hostility between the United States and Germany. President Wilson decided to publish the document, no doubt with British approval, and five weeks after the telegram was published, in April 1917, the United States declared war on Germany.

Although covert intelligence has its special appeal, it is not necessarily the most useful. Commonly available sources of information can be equally important. For instance, international weather reports may lead to agricultural forecasts which might affect Canadian wheat sales or perhaps the stability of a foreign government. Much ingenious work was put into such mundane things, leading to interesting political assessments. The secret about these sorts of activities is how they are done and what use is made of them.

Information is the grist of the diplomatic mill and, in the decades after World War II, getting it began with reading newspapers. Reading a paper, like riffling through intelligence or any other kind of report, became a skill to be developed according to the nature of the job at hand. In a democracy, it was particularly important to know what people were reading to understand what attitudes were likely to be encountered, particularly in Parliament. Preparing answers for the minister to questions likely to be asked in the House was always a high priority in the Department. Questions could usually be anticipated by watching the news media.

Trying to influence what gets into the media or to use the media in support of a diplomatic operation is a logical extension of reading the news. The idea of managing the news upsets the media, although everyone with any interests to promote or protect has tried to do it at least overtly by issuing press releases, giving interviews or paying for advertisements. By the sixties and seventies, the other method, cooking the news, was not as easy as it once had been. Communications were too good and one version of events could be checked against another before any drastic conclusions were reached. The Department was never very good at press relations, although they were greatly improved while Trudeau was in office.

The Canadian Press news agency was notoriously reluctant to send expensive foreign correspondents abroad. Instead, the CP distributed the offerings of the Associated Press, whose reporters had an entirely American readership in mind as they wrote. Fortunately, there were other sources of information, particularly the CBC, which allowed Canadians to see the world through Canadian eyes. The cheap and easy way, in this as in many other things, meant that it became increasingly difficult for anyone depending on the press for information to distinguish between Canadian interests and American interests. Foreign policies that were based on the same perceptions would tend to be the same. Consequently an independent foreign policy aimed at serving Canada's interests depended — and still depends — on its citizens having their own Canadian sources of information.

Consider Pierre Trudeau's famous comment that he could get all the information he needed about the world from reading the *New York Times*. It was, no doubt, a throw-away remark, but it did put the Department on the defensive over its role as political reporter. His was not the only question raised about the value of diplomatic reports in an age when there was more information available than there was time to use it.

Diplomatic reporting had much in common with journalistic reporting, the most important difference being that the journalist's object was to get his stuff as widely read as possible, while the diplomat wrote for a small, identified readership on precisely identified subjects. Most of the information contained in diplomatic reports would have been obtained on an understanding that it would be protected — i.e., that it would only be made available to the people in the diplomat's government who had a need to know. (Incredibly, there were people naïve enough to expect that information given to a diplomat was for his own personal edification and that it would not be reported home.) The result was that there was more candour between diplomats and their sources than there could be between journalists and theirs. There was also more candour between diplomatic reporters and their readers, which made it more fun (and less inhibiting) to write diplomatic reports than newspaper pieces. Diplomats could, indeed had to, identify sources, gossip properly labelled as such was acceptable and spades could be called spades without fear of libel.

Because information was so important to them, governments spent a good deal of money acquiring it, quite apart from their intelligence budgets. Diplomatic representation allowances were partially justified by the information they brought into the system. Cocktail parties, the bane of diplomatic life, were simply marketplaces where information was acquired and paid for in whisky and in kind. Dinner parties were much the same, but provided an opportunity to go into things in greater depth. This is not to say that every cocktail or dinner paid for itself in terms of information received, but it was the best way for diplomats to check impressions with others who had similar interests. Diplomatic functions enabled one to hear by way of gossip things that could be followed up in a more formal and organized way.

Most people would say things in a social and mildly alcoholic environment that they never would while sitting behind their own desks. Moreover, when it was necessary to make a point without making a formal démarche, to draw attention to something without putting it on record, quite unpalatable things could be passed on to a person at a cocktail party that couldn't be said to a foreign official in his own office without giving offence. Replies could be given in the same way.

The best diplomatic reports were highly selective and directed to specific issues known to be of interest to the government at home. They did not require the seeker after information to read between the lines or to wade through irrevalencies. The best would incorporate an analysis of what the issue was as seen from the embassy's vantage point, frequently quite different from the Ottawa view. Not all of the Department's diplomatic reports were good. Many were pointless, self-absorbed and pretentious. The diplomatic reporter is not like a journalist, who finds out quickly when his stuff is not being read. The Department was never very good about guiding its reporters. It was a recurring complaint of missions abroad that the correspondance all seemed to be one way. But there was never any question of the Department and its missions abroad trying to compete with a daily newspaper. On the other hand no newspaper, and especially not the *New York Times*, could pretend to provide the sort of information a Canadian government needed to conduct a Canadian foreign policy.

Mr Trudeau no doubt handed on the Canadian intelligence operation more or less as he had received it from his predecessor. With the Cold War still controlling the international climate, it would have been irresponsible to have tried to change it even if there had been any inclination in that direction. The situation for the military, however, was different, at least at the outset of the Trudeau era when all options were open, including that of neutrality. Trudeau's relations with the Canadian armed forces could never have been cordial, and it would be hard for anyone to judge how much respect the military could have mustered for one who had shown every sign of having shared the views of the people he associated with at the time, i.e., that World War II, being yet another imperial war, was none of his business.

For his part, before he left office, Trudeau might well have acquired some respect for an organization that was able to serve his government as effectively as the Canadian armed forces did, particularly after the invocation of the War Measures Act in 1970. Moreover, he might have acknowledged that the armed forces were the currency in which the Canadian government paid for its membership in some of the more influential international clubs like Nato and the Conference on Security and Cooperation in Europe (CSCE), set up by the Helsinki Accord which Trudeau signed on behalf of Canada in 1975.

So far as the Department was concerned, the long-standing and sometimes uneasy relationship between it and National Defence was not affected by changes in leadership. In its formative years, the Department's main role had been to support the armed forces in fighting the 1939–1945 war by cultivating allies, competing for scarce military supplies and providing political support in their struggle to retain a degree of independence from Allied embraces.

With the coming of peace, the roles were reversed and the armed forces became a diplomatic instrument, a part of the resources available to the government in its international dealings. They had some internal functions in maintaining law and order but it was in international matters that the Department of National Defence and External normally came into contact.

The Department probably dealt more often with National Defence than with any other department except Trade and Commerce. Defence policy and foreign policy have a *yin–yang* relationship: one begins where the other leaves off and neither can have an existence that is totally independent of the other. When both were operating on the same wavelength, the relationship was easy and profitable, but because of the angles from which they looked at issues, especially on subjects of shared responsibility (nuclear weaponry, the Vietnam operation) disagreements occured and they could be bitter.

Although it was not fashionable to say so, Canada's security situation was unique to it, quite distinct from that of its superpower neighbours to the south and to the north. During the Cold War, our land, sea and air spaces were of the utmost strategic importance to the great military rivals who were physically separated largely by Canadian space. Neutrality, as was learned in the early Trudeau days, was not an option for Canada simply on the grounds that it did not have the resources to defend its vast spaces against all comers in all circumstances. This fact more than any other had been behind Canada's enthusiasm for Nato, which provided a framework for mutual defence with other countries, especially with our dominant neighbour to the south. Most Canadian governments since the thirties had based Canada's defence posture on the assumption that the United States had to defend Canada whether it wanted to or not, while Canada had no hope of defending itself against the United States. This was a cheap and effective defence policy so long as the Soviet Union was the only obvious enemy, but there was no rigorously honest examination of what the consequences were for leaving one's defences up to another country and no serious attempt was made to see if there could be a different way of ensuring Canada's security.

This quintessentially Canadian approach to the country's security requirements had many tangled historical roots. Unlike most countries, Canada had been blessed by never having had to shed blood either for independence or in revolution. Such fighting as Canada had seen was in defending its territory from American attack in the 1770s and in the War of 1812. Thereafter it had participated in British imperial adventures of the nineteenth and twentieth centuries (more or less for the hell of it, certainly not in the defence of any clear-cut Canadian national interest) and, since 1939, had acted as a conscientious member of an international order that was itself under attack.

Much of Canada's military tradition was vicarious. The late, lamented Royal Canadian Navy did its damnedest to identify itself with the Royal Navy and carried its efforts to such extremes that it just about destroyed itself. Certainly it had few friends in the Canadian establishment to respond to its cry for help on the occasion of the integration of the armed forces in the 1960s. The Permanent Force Army had similar attitudes, although its experiences in World War II changed them. In spite of a historical British background and an inherited preference for British practices over American (especially in their attitudes toward things like rum rations) the Canadian Army was far from an uncritical admirer of "the Imperials." The Royal Canadian Air Force, of the three services in World War II, was less enthusiastically British if only because it had less luck in separating itself from British management than either of the other services.

The net result was that, although their personnel were sometimes admired as individuals and for the respect their achievements brought to the country, the main historic role the Canadian armed forces played in the collective life of Canada was as a bone of contention, specifically over the matter of conscription. In Israel, for instance, the Defence Force was essential to the survival of the state and was regularly called upon to prove the point. As a conscript service, it also played a vital part in building an Israeli nationality. Immigrant Jews from all over the world, speaking dozens of languages, were obliged to serve in the IDF, which operated exclusively in the Hebrew language.

In the United States, members of the armed forces and the veterans in the American Legion personified American nationalism. The US armed forces had played an indispensible part in creating the country, in keeping it together through the Civil War, in expanding its territories westward and southward and in extending its influence beyond its boundaries, first in the Spanish–American war and then in World Wars I and II and in the many lesser wars that have followed. "National security," the most potent rallying cry in American politics, has always meant the armed forces. No one, particularly a military person, could fail to be impressed by the prestige accorded the US forces in their own country.

While the Department was loosening the British connection during the early postwar years, the Canadian armed forces did not immediately follow suit. Only gradually, through participation in Nato and Norad, both of which were under heavy influence from the United States, did the Canadian military role models move westward. The process of co-operation, including sharing integrated command structures with the Americans, particularly in Norad, preceded the unification of Canada's armed forces; however, unification no doubt speeded up the process. It seemed as if the quasi-colonial relationship that Canada's military had had with Britain was simply being transferred to the United States.

Here again, history was at work. Canadian governments had come to rely on others to do their strategic thinking and even to take on other jobs (sea and air surveillance, for instance) required for the defence of Canadian space. Canada's armed forces were never given identifiable national objectives that were uniquely their own and the resources they would have needed to perform them. By and large, they were always a part of some external body for all purposes except the thankless law-and-order work at home. That, and the absence of any nation-building role, could only reinforce the long-standing tendencies of our armed forces to look abroad for inspiration. The people in the armed forces were as Canadian as anyone else but they were never given a part to play in the nation's life that could appeal to the imagination of the country as a whole. Even the role of protecting sovereignty in the Arctic was left mostly to the RCMP. On the other hand, they were regularly exposed to the nationalisms and military cultures of their dominant allies, which they could easily adopt as their own.

Thus, while the military in most countries see themselves as the custodians, or at least the symbols, of their country's nationalism-patriotism, it was possible for members of the Canadian military to see themselves first and foremost as members of an alliance or, on occasion, as representatives of an international organization. In Cyprus, for instance, Canadian officers under UN command have refused to give information to Canadian respresentatives on the grounds that they were working for the UN and that any information Ottawa wanted should be obtained through the Canadian delegation in New York! It was admirable and said a great deal that is good about this country, but it was not a reaction that would have been expected from officers of other countries in the same position.

Along the same lines, in the early seventies, during the period of the ascendency of Messrs Haldeman and Ehrlichman in Nixonian Washington, American withdrawal from Vietnam was on the agenda, with all that meant in emotional terms to the American military establishment. There had been wild speculation about how the US armed forces would react to an order to pull out of Indochina. A senior officer on the Joint Staff in Washington, in effect a Canadian military attaché, was asked how he thought his American counter-parts would take an order to withdraw from Vietnam. It took a while for him to take the question on board; that he was being asked by a Canadian official to assess US military morale and its willingness to obey a difficult order. When he was sure he'd understood the question, his reply was curt: "I don't spy on allies." Only a team-playing Canadian would give an answer like that. Military attachés are licensed intelligence agents, among other things, and certainly an American equivalent in Ottawa would have had a ready answer to an equivalent question put to him.

In the same way, in 1973 Canada's involvement in the not-so-new and unimproved armistice supervisory arrangements in Vietnam was seen by some of the military people taking part as an extension of our alliance with the United States. They were there to help the Americans carry out their policy in Indochina. Accordingly, they had little sympathy for those in the Department who saw no compelling Canadian interest being served by our continued presence in Vietnam. Yet it did not take a lawyer to see that neither Nato nor Norad applied to Southeast Asia. Indeed, it could be argued that continued US involvement in Vietnam adversely affected both alliances.

The Vietnam war also gave rise to some emotional conflict within the Canadian armed forces, a result of many years of collaboration with their American colleagues who were fighting and dying in that grisly mess. Some clearly felt Canada should have been fighting there too. One senior Canadian officer who was actively involved in setting up Canadian participation in the ICCS had had a son killed serving with the Americans in Vietnam.

All things considered, it is little wonder that the cool detachment inspired by Trudeau and adopted by the Department struck no corresponding chord in National Defence. No doubt, some of the armed forces' interest in the ICCS could be attributed to the opportunity it gave them to be of help to their American colleagues and, no doubt, some information acquired in our international role found its way to Washington. But that was not the policy, it was in spite of it.

The role of the military attaché, the licensed spy mentioned above, is a very special one. During the Cold War there was a working arrangement among Nato MAs, particularly in Iron Curtain countries. MAs were accredited directly to the military chief of staff of the host country and in most countries they formed a small diplomatic corps of their own. Occasionally their tasks could create minor embarrassments for a head of post but in other circumstances their entrée into otherwise closed circles in the host country was extremely valuable.

The most frequent contacts many Canadian missions abroad had with the armed forces were visits from naval vessels and from the National Defence College. That institution was the only place in Canada where senior military, public servants, academics and business persons came together to think about international politics, including the problems of peace and security in the broadest sense. Their tours, like the visits of Canadian ships, often added a new dimension to the contacts our missions abroad had in the host countries.

Still, none of these peripheral activities was a substitute for a defence policy which, during the Trudeau years and before, boiled down to doing the minimum necessary as a member of Nato and Norad, participating in peacekeeping operations and providing aid to the civil authority. The Department of National Defence Annual Report for 1977 does go further, but the actual resources made available, not the government's statements of policy, determined what was done, and DND was far down in the queue for available funds. For instance, when the vast continental shelf off the shores of Canada's three oceans became Canada's responsibility to manage it doubled overnight the area the navy was expected to cover. No additional resources were provided to match the new responsibility.

As already mentioned, early in the Trudeau government's life, all options, including the idea of neutrality, were declared open, and Canada's military presence in Europe was ordered reduced. It was done before the foreign policy review had been completed and was intended to show that the new government was serious about being different. As no thought had been given to its total foreign policy context, the gesture ran counter to other foreign policy objectives the government had in Europe. It might have been expected that people who were thinking in terms of placing a control on American economic penetration of Canada under the Third Option would also have thought of the need this would create for preserving a symbol of Canada's continuing interest in Europe. Naturally, the Europeans took the reduction of Canadian forces in Europe as a sign of diminished Canadian interest there. A few years later, when the message finally got back to an older and wiser government, the Contractual Link negotiation had to be undertaken as a special effort to extract Canada from the American economic basket where the Europeans had consigned it. The Department's involvement in the decision to move troops out of Europe was at best nominal, but it was very heavily involved in subsequent damage control activities.

The notion of neutrality that the Trudeau administration had floated in its early days did not survive examination by a travelling parliamentary committee. Among other places, the committee went to Stockholm to look into the Swedish version of neutrality as an alternative to continuing membership in Nato. As the embassy in Stockholm went about lining up parliamentarians, bureaucrats and military people to talk to the Canadian visitors, it became clear that the idea of Canada imitating Swedish neutrality filled most of the Swedes the committee approached with horror. Neutrality in war, the Swedes said, presupposed two sides between which an armed neutrality could be declared and enforced. In World War II Sweden had learned to its sorrow that it was impossible for it to maintain real neutrality after the Nazis had taken control in Norway, Denmark and most of the Baltic coastline. To their great embarrassment, the Swedes found that they were militarily unable to resist German demands, specifically for the passage of German troops through Sweden to relieve the German garrisons in Norway. In the circumstances, Swedish neutrality was nothing more than a convenience for Germany.

The Swedish participants in the briefings for the Canadian MPs made polite noises about neutrality being a matter for Canada to decide, but then proceeded to say how vital it was that neutrality be enforceable. Consequently, they stressed, neutrality did not mean less attention to defence, but more. It was not, they said, the cheapest form of defence but the most expensive. It was also the most difficult, because it made it made it necessary for Sweden to have its own arms industry to ensure a supply of weapons and munitions in circumstances when other suppliers would be most reluctant to deliver them. One Swedish Conservative politician made a further point. Sweden did not regard Nato as a potential enemy, he said; quite the contrary. In the event of war Sweden would want Nato to win. If Sweden joined Nato, he said, it would become a prime target for the Warsaw Pact forces and a strategic liability to Nato. As a well-armed neutral, however, Sweden could guarantee that its territory would not be used against Nato and thus leave Nato free to use its forces elsewhere. Thus, he said, being armed and neutral was the greatest service Sweden could offer Nato.

The visit to Sweden just about finished the case for those who were advocating neutrality "on the Swedish model." The Swedish model if applied to Canada would have required an ability to convince both the United States and the Soviet Union that neither party would be able to use Canadian territory for aggressive purposes without first defeating a well-equipped and determined Canadian military machine. It only needed to be stated to be dismissed.

The "Swedish model" idea was a product of the Canadian peace movement, a heterogenous group which, during the fifties, sixties and seventies, earned enough respect that no government spokesperson was inclined to take it on directly. A principled objector to war is a formidable opponent and even the right of self-defence is very hard to support if it is going to lead to a nuclear holocaust. Nevertheless, it might not be a very great exaggeration to say that during the sixties and seventies, the peace movement as a whole certainly helped Canadian governments to avoid the enunciation of a defence policy that they were actually prepared to fund and carry out in practice. It was easier for governments to keep "winging it" on the defence front for as long as possible.

This having been said, there was a great deal of intellectual dishonesty among those in the peace movement. Those who argued that the price of a destroyer could and should be translated into dollars and sent in aid to their favourite developing country missed the point, probably deliberately. The starting assumption was that the destroyer served no useful purpose and would not be missed, but the basis of that assumption was never discussed. Destroyers and aid were both necessary ingredients in Canadian foreign policy, even if the balance between the two might well have been debated.

In spite of the casual way in which the Canadian armed forces were treated by governments when their services were not in demand, when they were called upon to perform, their high professionalism and morale were admired both at home and abroad. Canadian troops have been widely accepted as peacekeepers, respected for their human qualities as well as their professional effectiveness; wherever they've been used they've shown themselves to be resourceful and courageous.

The Department's view of the armed forces was never one of unmixed admiration, and vice versa. The most important differences External had with National Defence were less a matter of objectives than of attitudes toward both allies and presumed enemies. International "friendships" are ephemeral things that depend on many circumstances. It was just as important to keep in touch with "enemies" as it was with "friends." The self-styled "simple soldier man" liked to know with some certainty where people stood; diplomats liked to see things fluid. Although the relationship was often difficult, diplomacy was defence by other means and defence was what gave diplomacy its ultimate sanction.

These were not, however, the sorts of principles on which Prime Minister Trudeau operated. Although his cool detachment was noted and absorbed by the Department, like the sideburns of its members that rose and fell with those of the PM, it was more a matter of style than of principle. In the same way, Trudeau's interest in management techniques had little effect on his own *modus operandi,* which was to fly by the seat of his pants. Indeed, the state of the country up to the Quebec referendum of 1980 could hardly have been managed otherwise, and the country was fortunate to have a Pierre Trudeau at the controls.

9

Exit Trudeau with Gestures

For the Department's agents abroad most of the Trudeau era, upbeat in so many ways, was marred by a feeling expressed by many of the foreigners they dealt with that Canada might be disintegrating. The FLQ crisis of 1970–71 was followed by the election of an avowedly separatist government in Quebec in 1976. Then came the referendum of 1980, and even after the "Non" vote those who followed events in Canada were treated to yet more rounds of constitutional wrangling. The proposition contained in *Foreign Policy for Canadians* that foreign policy is the extension of domestic policies into the foreign environment applied with a vengeance to internal disunity, reducing the ability to deal with international issues on their own merits.

In the mid to late seventies, most foreign countries had the impression that Canada was in narcissistic disarray. Canadian diplomats put a good deal of their energy into trying to persuade concerned foreigners and expatriate Canadians that Canada was still in business and was likely to remain so. Its representatives turned up at all the usual international gatherings and said and did what Canada was expected to say and do, but the old self-confidence, slipping over into self-righteousness, wasn't there. The government's foreign development assistance programme, for instance, was distinctly skewed in some parts of francophone Africa by domestic Canadian considerations. The rest of the world knew that Canadian unity had been challenged and indeed that another country, France, had taken a considerable hand in doing just that.

The perennial search for the perfect Canadian constitution and its patriation in 1982 also puzzled foreigners who have since learned, perhaps, that the search for an identity is part of Canada's identity. Just as many of them were coming to accept as fact that Canada was, indeed, an independent country capable of having a foreign policy of its own, we seemed to be behaving as if this might not be entirely true. Our untidy constitutional links with Britain, by then almost forgotten, once again came to the fore when we asked the British Parliament to approve our revised constitution. The addition of a Charter of Rights and Freedoms was open to the construction that in some way Canadians had not had these rights and freedoms before. All the attention given to domestic affairs inevitably dimmed the image of the brave Middle Power doing things that needed to be done on the international scene and replaced it with the picture of a nervous country absorbed by its own problems.

For a time it was only in the Commonwealth that Canada was playing an active multilateral role. Trudeau's first encounter with the Commonwealth had been at the Heads of Government meeting in London in 1969. He later reinforced the link by becoming a champion of its Third World member countries. Because he was able to focus attention on the problems of its less privileged members Trudeau is usually credited with making the Commonwealth a stronger institution, sometimes over the objections of its British founders. Part of Trudeau's attraction to the Commonwealth was the format of the Heads of Government gatherings, which provided occasions for politicians to talk to politicians without bureaucratic interference about the science of government — e.g., about how to fire an unwanted cabinet minister. Trudeau tried to transform la Francophonie into something like the Commonwealth but failed because France, unlike Britain in the Commonwealth, regarded la Francophonie as a useful instrument of French policy and was not about to permit that to be changed.

Under Trudeau, the Department had a number of ministers, some almost transitory. After Mitchell Sharp's five-year tenure, he was succeeded by Allan MacEachen in 1974. Two years later, Don Jamieson, hitherto unknown for his international activity, became minister. Although he was well liked as a conscientious and sympathetic minister, his appointment was not taken as a great compliment to the Department. His concern to have people like him made him an uneasy negotiator. He was later appointed High Commissioner in London after the return of Trudeau from his brief retirement in 1980.

The defeat of the Liberal government in May 1979 had led to the most awkward transition period in recent Canadian history. Jamieson was succeeded by Flora MacDonald, who came to the job bearing the albatross of Joe Clark's promise to move the Canadian embassy in Israel from Tel Aviv to Jerusalem. Robert Stanfield was invoked as *deus ex machina*, to straighten that out.

During her brief tenure, Miss MacDonald wrote an extraordinary article for the Toronto *Globe and Mail* complaining that her Under-secretary, Allan Gotlieb, had done something scandalously improper by being in contact with other deputy ministers in what she regarded as an underhanded attempt to find out what had been decided in cabinet. Nothing could have better illustrated the decline in the status of the Department and its once unassailable chief. Shades of past mandarins — that the dialogue of deputy ministers, which had made Canadian governments function for decades, should be taken as something just short of treason! The government of Mr Clark collapsed shortly after and Flora MacDonald's views on how the Department ought to have been run were not further developed. There may have been more to Flora MacDonald's complaint than met the eye, but the article as it appeared was particularly puzzling to those who had known the days when the co-ordination of government operations depended on how well deputy ministers were plugged in with their colleagues.

On Trudeau's return in 1980, Mark MacGuigan became Secretary of State for External Affairs until his resignation two years later, when he was succeeded by Allan MacEachen for his second stint as minister. He left External for the Senate when John Turner became Prime Minister in June of 1984 and was replaced by Jean Chrétien, who departed when the Liberals were defeated by the Conservatives later that same year. This procession of six ministers in ten years through the Department was not calculated to improve its morale, which had already become a matter of public concern.

In August of 1980, while Trudeau's final departure from Ottawa was still four years off, media reports of dissatisfaction in the Department had become such that the government approved an Order-in-Council authorizing an inquiry into conditions in the Foreign Service. Dissatisfaction in External was not something unheard of. In its palmiest days the administration, the filing system and a dedication to close-fisted bookkeeping were enough to make most members discontented at one time or another. Although those particular grievances gradually disappeared, they were replaced by others. The political animals within the Department were seldom fervent admirers of the political animals in the "government of the day," but the Trudeau government had, in effect, demoted what had been an élite organization, a central government agency, into a department of government like any other. By 1980 departmental mutterings had reached the point where the government thought it necessary to do something about them.

The Order-in-Council setting up the one-person Royal Commission allowed that the material changes in the conditions of foreign service may not have been adequately recognized by the public servants who were managing it. There was a fear that the new level of discontent could lead "to a decline in the incentives for service abroad and affect the motivation that has underlain the high professional standards of the Foreign Service." Nothing specific was mentioned about the nature of these misgivings. However, the clearest indication that something was wrong would have been a falling off in recruitment — fewer high-grade applicants and more rejections of job offers by those who topped the eligibility list. It seems likely that the brightest and best university graduates were going elsewhere. If so, since the FS competition was the prime attraction for the public service generally, a change of this sort would be quickly noticed.

Pam McDougall, then Deputy Minister of Health and Welfare, formerly Inspector-General of the Foreign Service and once Ambassador to Poland, was appointed as the one-woman Royal Commission to find out what was wrong and recommend how to set it right. In his letter outlining her terms of reference, the Prime Minister asked the Commissioner to look into the "dissatisfaction which seems to be prevalent in the foreign service" relating to the roles of the service and how they were *perceived* within and outside the service itself as well as the conditions of foreign service which might have contributed to the situation. Then the Prime Minister's letter added, "While your Study must deal with *perceptions of foreign service roles*, I must underline that it is not meant to be an inquiry into *the role* of the foreign service [italics provided]." The letter went on at some length saying, in effect, what the Prime Minister thought was wrong, most of which, the PM suggested, had to do with working conditions and personnel management matters.

The Commissioner's terms of reference permitted an examination of *perceptions of roles*, but excluded the actual *role* of the Foreign Service as it had been redefined by the Trudeau government. Obviously, no government would appoint a Royal Commission to look into how it conducted its foreign policy, but the exclusion of "the role" went further than that. It precluded the examination of the way the Foreign Service (and the Department in general) was being used (or not being used) by the government in the conduct of its foreign policy. It has been said that the greatest single source of human

dissatisfaction is an absence of meaning in one's life. The Royal
Commission was not authorized to look into that essential aspect of
the Department's malaise.

It wasn't that there was a lack of work for Canadian diplomats.
There had been, among other things, the challenge of applying the
Third Option, the collapse of détente, the development of the new
Asian and Pacific Rim relationship and the need for a new link with
the EC. People who are busy doing what they think is an important
job in a good cause do not make an issue out of the physical discom-
fort of a fourth floor walk-up in Beijing, nor would they quit the
career, or not join it, because its rigours had never been reflected
very handsomely in the allowances they were paid. The dissatisfaction in the Foreign Service was not caused by grievances of this sort.
It was a by-product of the absence of a role that could challenge the
sort of people the Foreign Service courted and recruited.

The Department was no longer the primary source of information
and advice on matters of foreign policy. It was no longer a decisive
element in the diplomatic process and certainly not the exclusive
instrument through which the government's foreign policy was conducted abroad. Under Trudeau, members of the government or of the
Prime Minister's Office were frequent travellers abroad; telephone
calls between Ottawa and Washington, without reference to the embassy, continued or increased. The Department had become a communications system at the disposal of the government. It might well
be that the Department was not performing to the Prime Minister's
satisfaction or that he had a different concept of how diplomacy
should be conducted. Nevertheless, it was the diminished role assigned to the Department by the government, justifiable or not, that
was the source of the dissatisfaction that the Royal Commission was
set up to investigate. But the terms of reference the Prime Minister
set for Pam McDougall precluded any examination of that loss of
role. In effect she was asked to do a study of the administration and
management of the foreign service. She did a very good one.

The Royal Commission report pinpointed many long-standing
employee grievances and suggested ways of removing them, but it
could not discuss the main reason for the disenchantment. Highly
qualified and motivated young Canadians were being sought out,
hired, maintained and paid to go through motions which only by
coincidence could be seen as influencing government policy. Race-
horses, which was what the government was still hiring for the
Department, become restive if they are used for delivering milk.

Pierre Trudeau had publicly deprecated the Department's reporting role, and others in the Prime Minister's Office had wondered
aloud whether foreign relations could not be conducted by the domestic departments responsible for the subject at hand, co-ordinated
as necessary by themselves. This denial of diplomacy as a craft in
its own right was common. Clearly, in these minds the conduct of
foreign relations was not qualitatively different from any other business of government. Many in the business were asked what they did
that was so important but few who had asked the question waited for
or listened to the answer. In any case, a fully satisfactory answer
required more time and a broader background knowledge than the
questioners had at their disposal. As usual, the truth was in the
details.

Consider the following. An important decision is about to be taken
by a foreign government that would adversely affect Canadian interests. The diplomatic mission in the country concerned must first get
wind of it at an early stage, then inform the government at home of
what is happening and seek instructions on what should be done
about it (usually offering suggestions). The right person to approach
in the foreign government apparatus has to be identified, he or she
has to be persuaded to meet with Canadian representatives (when he
or she might well prefer not to) and a case has to be prepared in
accordance with instructions from Ottawa that the foreign government could use, probably in public, to justify changing its mind.
Consideration would also be given to the possible consequences of
a failure to change the offending policy, including retaliation. The
Canadian diplomatic mission must discover how to let the foreign
government know of the possibilities without seeming to threaten
and how to advise and warn Ottawa of the chances and consequences
of failure.

To do this job requires a combination of local knowledge at the
personal, cultural, political, economic and historical level. It also
calls for tradecraft, the details of how to go about things, and that is
acquired only by experience.

A decent representative serving abroad must therefore know how
decisions are made and communicated at home and abroad. He
should have had enough practice in using the system, or in seeing it
used, to be able to judge how far he can go on his own and when he
must seek advice and support from home. These skills are not picked
up by doing other things, by reading the literature or even by getting
elected to Parliament, but it is not easy to explain that to one whose

starting position is that there is nothing about diplomacy that a smart, businesslike manager couldn't pick up as he went along. Where largely unpredictable circumstances play such an important part in matters of fundamental importance, surely there must be an indisputable need for a profound knowledge of the trade that can only be acquired by a long period of training and apprenticeship.

There was no one close to Pierre Trudeau who would accept such a proposition. The view of the diplomat as an overpaid messenger persisted in Ottawa and continued to influence the way the government's foreign operations were eventually reorganized. The Interdepartmental Committee for External Relations (ICER) in the early seventies gradually became the principal instrument for co-ordination abroad, a role that once had been External's principal raison d'être. Although the Undersecretary was ICER's chairman and the Department provided its secretary, External Affairs was just another member of the Committee. In theory it had no more to say about what resources would be used abroad and for what purposes than any other member of the Committee. It certainly was in no position either to arbitrate or to lay down the law. In its operation (because public servants have a way of making improbable things work) ICER was not the source of paralysis it might have been and its members were able to carry on their separate operations pretty much as they always had, in spite of it. There were some positive aspects as well. Consultation, always a problem, became assured under ICER; anyone who had a reason for being kept informed could insist on information and get it. The allocation of resources to competing operations had, at last, a mechanism for getting that difficult job done.

Unfortunately ICER was not viewed by the rationalizers as an end in itself but as a means toward the total integration, not just of the different foreign services, but of the different, sometimes conflicting, always competing Canadian operations abroad. In retrospect, what was wanted was an ultimate solution to what seemed to the management experts as an unnecessary complication of jurisdictions. What they ignored was that the system that had evolved did, in truth, reflect the realities of international life and the conflicting and competing Canadian interests in it. Each of the major interests had its own champion and External, with no competing programmes of its own, was there to bring them all into co-ordination. The ICER solution made External into one of the competitors.

Members of External who were involved with the ICER process and its exhausting interdepartmental budgeting sessions came to have a reluctant admiration of that process. But the most important result was that a super-department for foreign affairs became the logical next step. The majority in the Department had confidently assumed that the super-department, if it came, would be a more efficient way for External Affairs to do its job of co-ordinating and interweaving all the various strands of Canada's interests abroad into one strong and consistent line of action. In short, the assumption in External was that the foreign policy component would dominate in the new super-department-to-be. Only a wise minority foresaw what actually happened.

On January 12, 1982, Prime Minister Trudeau announced the creation of the new foreign ministry to be responsible for the bulk of Canada's operations abroad. The new creation incorporated all of External Affairs, much of the Department of Trade and Commerce, including its Foreign Trade Service, and the foreign operations side of the Department of Immigration as well as that of the Canadian International Development Agency. Canada's foreign services were thus brought under one roof, although separate career lines were created for the former External, Trade, Immigration, and CIDA foreign service personnel. Information and administrative services were fully integrated. It all seemed very logical and destined to strengthen Canada's hand in the international environment by allowing it to concentrate such diplomatic clout as Canada had at its command and allow the government to deal with the international community through a single agency. It seemed to be the culmination of a process that went back to the very beginning of Canada's appearance on the international scene as a power of some consequence.

A super-department under the co-ordinating influence of the "political" element in the former External Affairs would have had the potential to be an effective diplomatic instrument for the protection and advancement of all of Canada's interests abroad. Subject to the usual compromises and the will of the government, the "functional" and "political" elements could have supported each other in the effort to attain Canada's broad objectives in the international community. But this was not what happened. Instead, the old External Affairs "political" element was left with the issues in which Canada's direct interests were not involved while the main thrust of our international activity was directed by the "functional" experts, mainly those concerned with international trade.

This is no criticism of the Foreign Trade Service. Under the new arrangement they would go on doing what they were created to do, sell our exports, but they would do it with less input from what was left of the External "political" element. Indeed, judging from what could be seen from the outside, the input was from the other side and the new super-department became an instrument of commercial policy. The protection and advancement of Canada's broader interests was subordinated to the shorter-term interests of the business community.

The Department's Annual Report for 1982–83 should have been enough to give pause to any who were still in doubt. After a brief history of the measures that began with the publication of *Foreign Policy for Canadians* in 1970, the Report went on to note in appropriately twisted syntax that since the early seventies, "Canada's national objectives have shifted towards economic emphasis."

The new department would be presided over by the Secretary of State for External Affairs, "charged with managing the broad mandate" of the super-department, but with two other ministers "with more precisely defined responsibilities," one of which was International Trade. The second was a Minister for External Relations, responsible mostly for cultural affairs and international development assistance. All three were of cabinet rank and, as such, each of them had the power, if they chose to use it, to carry their disagreements to cabinet.

For such a three-headed monster to survive, it would be essential that the vast majority of its conflicts be settled in-house, before they went to cabinet. As public servants know well, cabinet ministers do not like being asked to settle routine disputes between bureaucrats. Consequently, the traditional conflicts between the broad overarching considerations of foreign policy and the interests of the specialist groups would simply have to be settled within the super-department, which was organized to get that job done at the lowest possible level. Those responsible for Canadian operations abroad (trade, information, development, immigration) and experts in something called "general relations" were combined within geographical divisions. As a result, not only routine disputes about "turf" but fundamental policy differences which might otherwise be brought to cabinet would never get there. At worst they could be settled by middle-grade public servants; at best the triumvirate of ministers would agree on something they could all live with. This would be tolerable, even laudable, if someone responsible for the overview function once exercised by External would have the last word before cabinet. There is no evidence that this was the way it worked.

The emphasis on managerial considerations and the centralization of responsibility that was the hallmark of the Trudeau administration left the Department and its professional diplomats outside the mainstream of foreign policy decision making for the first time since the 1940s. This may have been an objective of the tortuous processes of the seventies, although it is hard to know for sure, since no one ever acknowledged that changing departmental roles or increasing centralization was any part of the managerial revolution.

The transformation of the Department that took place in 1982 had been the climax of a long period of uprooting, self-examination and reorganization which left it with little energy for much else. One way and another, very little of what was done on the international scene in the name of Canada between 1980 and 1984 could have borne the imprint of the Department, including Pierre Trudeau's final foray into the field of disarmament.

In a speech made in Canada in October 1983, a few months before his final retirement, the Prime Minister returned to foreign affairs to leave his personal mark on the world scene. He chose the world's most pressing problem, the threat of a nuclear holocaust. After a brief bow in the direction of détente, the process that had begun with the signing of the Helsinki Accord in 1975 and had been ended by the Soviet invasion of Afghanistan in December of 1979, the Prime Minister then zeroed in on arms reduction as the key to world peace. He was badly advised. As the head of the government of a country whose allies thought it was carrying less than its share of the military burden and as a person who was not known as a student of military affairs, he was ill-placed to preach on that politically, economically, emotionally and technically loaded subject. More important, he had nothing to offer in the process of negotiation. Canada was only a member of the international disarmament community by virtue of the part it had played in the development of the original atomic bomb fifty years before, by the fact that Canada had the capacity to become an atomic power in its own right, and by the Department's ability to see that Canadian delegations pulled their weight in the disarmament committees' work. By 1983 these qualifications had worn very thin.

The Prime Minister seemed to have been relying on his personal reputation as a tough and realistic speaker of unpalatable truths. He appeared to hope that once he had laid bare the idiocy of the arms race and presented a mechanism and a timetable for further action, the leaders of the international community, particularly the leaders of the United States and the Soviet Union, would see the error of their ways, welcome his sensible suggestions and begin to implement them.

No disarmament process of any significance has ever worked simply because it should have. Where any has worked it has been driven either by economic considerations or by a change in the political atmosphere. Arming is a function of international tension, not the cause of it, although no doubt it adds to existing tension. The brutal fact is that in a community of sovereign states, a mix of the slogan of the US National Rifle Association and the Charter of UNESCO applies: "Guns don't start wars; wars begin in the minds of men." Until there is a world government that includes a legislature, a police force, courts with compulsory jurisdiction, and a means of coercing those found guilty, disarmament must begin with a change in the political atmosphere.

Trudeau was obviously attracted to the upside-down logic of those fine people who argued that if you converted swords into plough-shares the result would be peace. The Prophet Isaiah said quite the opposite — that if the rule of God were accepted then it would be possible to beat swords into ploughshares. He did not say that if swords were beaten into ploughshares, the peace of God would follow.

If he had been better advised, there was a theme that the Prime Minister could have promoted in the early eighties: to avoid a nuclear war, change the international climate and revive détente. It would have been consistent with Canada's military position in Nato and Norad and with its own history if the Prime Minister had urged governments to stop pursuing Cold War objectives in Afghanistan and elsewhere and get back to Helsinki where the machinery existed for settling disputes and for building confidence. He could have made unilateral gestures toward the USSR, as he had done before in the matter of China, and urged others to consider resuming the disrupted policy of détente. This might not have been considered timely by the United States, in particular, but it might well have hastened the moment that came in 1989 when the Soviet Union called off the Cold War (and the arms race) unilaterally, mostly for economic reasons. At the very least, anyone who had suggested a resumption of détente five years before it happened might have seemed prophetic and even a candidate for a Nobel Prize.

Not long after Trudeau's departure in 1984, political appointments to External became a matter of public controversy, to the point of drawing comment from the normally placid Professional Association of Foreign Service Officers (PAFSO), the Department's trade union. Some of these appointments were among the millstones Trudeau draped around the neck of John Turner on the occasion of his re-entering the political waters. The announcement that Bryce Mackasey was to be Canada's Ambassador to Lisbon irritated everyone concerned. First there was the question of announcing an ambassadorial appointment before the host government had agreed to accept the person nominated, an unnecessary lapse of international good manners. Then, although Mackasey had been around the Canadian political scene for quite a while, his qualifications as a diplomat were not obvious. The Portuguese government might well have wondered why they had been chosen. As a Canadian general election was called about the same time, Lisbon decided to wait and see what transpired. The government that had appointed Mackasey was defeated and the new government began repairing the damage done by withdrawing his nomination.

Pierre Trudeau's time at the head of the government of Canada has produced a great many books, and the treatment given him has not always been kind. He is the sort of person who excites controversy, an original with no easy comparisons who fits into no preconceived patterns and who has revealed so little of himself to so few people. The concern here is not to add to the Trudeau legend. Rather, it is to describe his use, disuse and misuse of what could and should have been a remarkable instrument in his hands, the Department of External Affairs that he inherited.

From the outset he distanced himself from his distinguished predecessor in a businesslike and unsentimental way. Then he made his advance to China in a bold and fresh approach to a perennial problem. By doing what was within the power of his own government to do, he did more than anyone else had in decades to bring the most populous country on earth back into the community of nations. By the end of his political career he was merely exhorting others to do things about the Cold War confrontation when there were sensible things that were within his government's own power to do if the people had been there to advise him and have their advice considered.

In everything he gave the air of a remote, detached, unemotional intelligence at the centre of a network of his own making, handing down decisions based either on his own ideas or on those of his chosen advisors. As a matter of courtesy, in which he excelled, he would accept briefing papers prepared for him by those constitutionally required to provide them, his cabinet colleagues, but there was usually another set of briefings, possibly attached to the official ones, geared to the Prime Minister's own interests, style and agenda.

His abiding interest was the machinery of government, including the constitution, and so far as the Department was concerned, his principal monument was the new super-department created in 1982. The idea of External as a central government agency was dead. The way the new super-department was set up ensured that economic considerations could effectively prevent what was left of the country's foreign affairs watchdog from barking, or being heard if it did. With no other governmental body specifically empowered to co-ordinate and harmonize the country's various interests abroad, the national interests of Canada were, in effect, equated with the bottom line of its immediate commercial interests. Not only would there be no body responsible for looking out for long-term interests abroad, economic and non-economic, but no body in the Ottawa apparatus would have a vested interest in bringing those considerations to cabinet attention.

In this situation, it is open to question whether the free trade deal of 1988 was ever presented to cabinet in either a historical context or in the context of the effects this new alignment would have on Canada's ability to take an independent position on principle where important American interests were at stake. It is hard to imagine how a paper that raised such questions could survive passage through the super-department to make its way to cabinet. All of this happened well after Trudeau left office, but his revisions of the External Affairs mandate would have served his successor's agenda very well indeed.

So Pierre Trudeau did not turn out to be the much-hoped-for leader under whose enlightened government the Department would conduct the diplomacy of perhaps the most strategically important space on the face of the earth. Instead, the Department's resources were used to further his designs in governmental management. Its mandate was changed from applying and policing the government's foreign operations to that of running its external machinery.

In making these changes, Trudeau facilitated the most significant foreign policy switch in Canadian history: the application of the Second Option, which his government had formally rejected on the grounds that it would inevitably lead to political as well as economic integration. The prediction that this "might be expected to generate opposition in Canada" turned out to be correct but inconsequential. No doubt these were not the intended results. It may have been assumed that those who followed Trudeau in office would not be so ideologically committed as to allow the country's foreign policy to be determined by economic considerations. Intentions to the contrary notwithstanding, the changes made in the role of the Department under Trudeau were of enormous help to those who succeeded him in having their way. Canada has assumed a different place in the world as a result.

Decision Times
1984 and All That

10

Zeitgeist

The Department that had been so neglected by Pierre Trudeau might have expected different things from John Turner, who was well known around Ottawa as an MP and as a minister in the Pearson, and later the Trudeau, cabinets. He had left the government in 1975 in circumstances that meant that he might not have shared all of Trudeau's interests and attitudes. However, the Turner project for External was not to be revealed. Instead, when Turner came back as Liberal leader and Prime Minister, he was quickly removed from office by a totally new phenomenon on the Canadian political scene. Brian Mulroney was a continentalist and an avowed believer in the inherent virtue of an uninhibited marketplace. The new Prime Minister was in tune with the spirit of the eighties, the *zeitgeist* exemplified by Margaret Thatcher and Ronald Reagan.

The 1940s had been dominated by World War II and its aftermath. The international concerns in the fifties had had to do with the Cold War: the creation of Nato and Norad, nuclear proliferation, competition in the exploration of outer space and the evolution of peacekeeping. The sixties saw a speeding up of decolonization and its consequences, especially an intensification of the Cold War with its hot spot in Vietnam where decolonization and the Cold War met. In Canada there had been the Centennial celebration, especially Expo 67, dampened by the growth of violence in Quebec.

The seventies, at least for the Department, had begun in optimism about affairs at home and abroad with a government led by an enlightened son of Quebec with a vision for the future of Canada. In that same decade, a separatist government was elected in Quebec while abroad, political and religious extremism, including terrorism, dominated the news. By the time the decade was out, the spirit of détente which had produced the Helsinki Accord of 1975 had been brought to an end by the Soviet incursion into Afghanistan.

For the so-called Western world the 1980s was to be the decade of economic readjustment, the scaling down of government interfer-

ence with business in favour of a free market. In Britain and the
United States most obviously, it was a time for the deregulation of
things like air transportation and the privatization of state-run enterprises. Business communities began to call the tune for government
and the open-handed social programmes that had been introduced in
earlier decades were reassessed. Abroad, both Mr Reagan and Mrs
Thatcher followed foreign policies that were more nationalistic and
assertive than those of their predecessors.

This was the international climate when Brian Mulroney won the
election in September of 1984 and came into office with the clear
intention of following in the well-blazed paths of the American and
British leaders. Unlike his models, however, he carried his business-
first attitude into the field of foreign affairs as well. He alone of the
new conservatives was not also a nationalist.

The super-department of External Affairs had its role to play, but
it was one that allowed little scope for independent gestures on the
international scene. The first changes came in the traditional cautious
relationship with the United States. Mulroney was the first prime
minister since Mackenzie King who could be remotely described as
pro-American. A few were the reverse and even King's high regard
for the United States had been tempered by a naturally suspicious
mind and a very broad streak of pragmatism.

The Mulroney approach to Canadian relations with the United
States is dealt with in devastating detail by Lawrence Martin in his
book *Pledge of Allegiance — The Americanization of Canada in the
Mulroney Years*. The book provides chapter and verse for those who
had any doubts about the change in direction. In the fifties there had
been people who thought the British knew best and that it was
presumptuous for Canada to venture out into the diplomatic world
by itself. In the eighties those who were inclined to think in this way
had pinned their faith on the wisdom of Washington.

American claims to leadership had always been passively acknowledged by Canadian governments, in the defence context especially,
but were rarely avowed, never stressed and certainly not welcomed in areas where defence was not the main issue. Under Mulroney this changed as he quickly concentrated on the issue of free
trade, a complete reversal of Trudeau's Third Option and a policy
that ten years earlier was seen as eventually leading to political
integration. After winning the election fought on this issue in 1988,
the Canada-US Free Trade agreement was ratified and the American

connection became broader and less conditional than it had ever been.

By 1989, the American invasion of Panama and the arrest of General Noriega, a one-time collaborator with the United States, on drug charges was gratuitously blessed by Canada. It was the sort of occasion when some Canadian governments of the past might actually have said something derogatory, if only to show how independent they were. This was the first government that would have thought it necessary to express approval. Canadian political attitudes were anticipating the emerging new economic relationship.

Mulroney appointed his predecessor, Joe Clark, whom he had unseated as head of the Progressive Conservative Party, to head the super-department of External Affairs and it was probably not his intention to enhance the importance of either. Although Clark went on to earn new respect in the job, the work that was left to him and to the Department was not of the first magnitude. While others conducted the vital negotiation of the Free Trade Agreement, Clark was left to handle matters like Southern Africa where no specifically Canadian interest was at stake. It was to Clark's credit (and perhaps the Department's as well) that he made the most of the work he was allowed to do.

Some of Mulroney's other appointments in the international field had different motives. The Mackasey affair, one of Trudeau's parting gifts to John Turner, had helped Mulroney defeat Turner; he learned from it that there were pitfalls to be avoided in making diplomatic appointments. Mulroney's choice of Stephen Lewis, a political personality as far removed philosophically from the government as could be found, to be Ambassador to the United Nations reflected what he had learned. Mr Lewis's qualifications for the job were very good but the government's reasons for appointing him no doubt had more to do with sanitizing future appointments than with the advancement of Canadian interests at the United Nations.

A comparable placatory offering was the far less obvious choice of Dennis McDermott as Ambassador to Ireland. A rough-and-ready trade union leader, he too was no political friend of the government that had appointed him but, unlike Stephen Lewis, he had shown no particular interest in foreign affairs.

There is something to be said in favour of a government appointing political friends to head diplomatic missions. The crony's knowledge of the domestic political scene and easy access to the people in power at home can be a great asset on a foreign post. That sort of insider knowledge and access can be important not only to the sending country but to the receiving one as well and can convey the idea that the country that sends a well-placed politician as its representative places a high value on the relationship. George Drew as High Commissioner in London had John Diefenbaker's ear and made use of it — often to the annoyance of the Department. The British, for their part, had every reason to be happy that Canada was sending a person of Mr Drew's influence to represent it in London. With one or two distinguished exceptions, the new Prime Minister's diplomatic appointments were not in the same category.

The translation of General John de Chastelain from Chief of the Defence Staff to Ambassador in Washington was in a class by itself. Sending a soldier to represent Canada in Washington no doubt said something about Brian Mulroney's perception of the new world order.

Mulroney's electoral success in 1984 obviously owed a lot to the strong reactions against Trudeau and his parting gestures but Mulroney's re-election in 1988 was entirely his own work. In both elections he was able to capitalize on a worldwide reaction against intrusive government — a dislike of economic regulation in times of prosperity and a growing sentiment in favour of letting the marketplace make decisions once made by politicians. There was also, no doubt, an element of the influence among Canadian voters of Ronald Reagan and the values for which he stood. All this represented something of a departure from what Conservatism had traditionally stood for in Canada, including what can only be called anti-Americanism. Although the process was a gradual one, by 1988 *laissez-faire* economics, once a Liberal principle, had become a Conservative cause and made the party more like the Republican Party in the United States than it had ever been before.

Perhaps the most important thing that happened to Canadian politics beginning in 1984 was that Canadian business for the first time got a government it could call its own. Not only was it ideologically friendly to business interests, but many of its members and much of its support came from the business community, which might well have considered that its turn was a long time coming. In foreign affairs, however, the correction went too far. The adoption of the entrepreneur's agenda left other vital national interests undefended. The debates that raged around the free trade issue during the election of 1988 concentrated on the agreement's commercial, social and cultural consequences, but this most significant foreign policy shift was not publicly discussed in those terms. No one seemed to wonder what effect the agreement would have on Canada's position in the world or even on our future political relationship with the United States. No one asked what the effect would be on Canada's ability to make independent choices if we put even more of our economic eggs in the American basket. The contrast with the position taken by a different government a mere ten years earlier, that the Second Option (closer economic alignment) would eventually lead to absorption, was barely mentioned. The argument was almost entirely about whether the benefits of the deal would be as great as its costs in economic terms. The rest had to do with its cultural impact.

If there had been a Department of External Affairs whose primary job was to watch over the totality of Canada's external interests, there would certainly have been at least a cabinet discussion of the effects the proposed new arrangement with the United States would have had on Canada's future ability to act independently. There might even have been some questions about its long-term effect on some cherished domestic programmes. If there had been a debate within the government on this aspect of the deal, almost certainly there would have been some echoes of it around Ottawa, in Parliament or in the election campaign. In the event, free trade was consistently treated as a commercial matter pure and simple, never as the major foreign policy shift that it was.

What advice might the Department have given the government while it was still looking at the idea of free trade? It isn't difficult to imagine what it might have said about how other countries, including the United States, would interpret the agreement in political terms. The Department might have noted some of the established attitudes toward Canada that exist within the international community. First, there would be a revival of the old reluctance of some foreigners to believe that Canada, considering its vitally important geopolitical position and its existing close economic and military links with the United States, could be a truly independent country. Those who wondered about Canada being an American cat's-paw would have wondered some more. And they would have had a point.

The disparity in the size of the partners has given the United States political and economic leverage here well beyond what it already had. It has been calculated that trade between Canada and the United States is some 200 times more important to the average Canadian than it is to the average American and that when push comes to shove, a Canadian government will be 200 times more sensitive to the consequences of a falling out than an American government would be. The Free Trade Agreement did not create the imbalance but, by enhancing the importance of trade between the two, it has multiplied its effect. No one can believe that with such leverage at its disposal, Washington will be able to resist the temptation to use it, and not only in economic matters. It will be more difficult for both partners to resist the urge to link together any of the whole range of issues that arise in the daily relationship between the two countries. This alone is an important break from the previous practice of dealing with issues on their own merits, when it would not have been possible, for instance, to make a concession on softwood lumber depend on a redefinition of Canadian content on TV. More than ever, Canada will be viewed, in the United States and elsewhere, as a part of the American system and we will be dealt with accordingly.

Free trade supporters drew a false analogy between the agreement's proposed elephant–mouse free trade area and that of the EC which consisted of twelve members, no two of which were economically strong enough to dominate the rest. Moreover, no one took the analogy far enough to ask if it would mean that Canada and the United States would, like the EC, have to move toward a common foreign policy.

In response, supporters of the free trade deal might say bluntly that it was sheer illusion to think that Canada could ever differ with the United States on any point of real importance. Canada, they might say, has never been able to disregard American interests and so nothing has been changed by the new arrangement.

No state, however powerful, has untrammelled power to do as it pleases; all are subject to restraints of one kind or another. Canada certainly has never been an exception to that. However, there is an important difference between a state that is a conscientious member of the international community that is a member of an alliance, and one that is a satellite. No one can deny that the Free Trade Agreement has further limited the degree of freedom Canada previously enjoyed in its dealings with the United States.

It is by its differences from the United States that Canada usually defines itself, internally as well as externally. Similarly, a rough indication of Canadian independence can be found in what our government does in matters of world importance in which the United States has a significant interest. For most Canadian governments, the indications will vary from the perversely different to the identical.

Under the Mulroney government the record has been almost without exception an identification with American positions.

The verdict of history is still to be rendered on the Coalition's expedition to the Persian Gulf in 1991. Nevertheless, it can safely be noted that it did not give birth to the long-awaited new world order that was to replace the global system of the Cold War. Even before the operations in the Gulf were ended there were reasons for believing that the Coalition's actions were ill-conceived, that this could have been seen at the time and that no attempt was made to point out the deficiencies. The unsatisfactory manner in which they were concluded confirmed most misgivings. Certainly any world order based on what happened in the Gulf would not be much of an improvement on the world order that preceded it; the direct use of overwhelming military power remained the decisive element and it was not followed by any meaningful remedial action.

This sort of assessment could have been made in the Department, as it was in the case of Korea when Canada successfully resisted the United States by insisting on having that war fought under the United Nations flag as a United Nations police action.

The face that Canada presents to the world is what enables Canadians of all cultures to recognize each other, particularly abroad, and to distinguish themselves from any other nationality. As the direction of our thinking moves from east and west to north and south, local economic interests take over from national ones and Canadians then begin to see themselves, not as a people with a special view of the world, but as components of their region of North America.

A central government agency looking after Canada's international interests as a whole could have warned the government about the effect of any further reduction in the degree of freedom this country had in its relations with the United States. Apart from the way it would alter other countries' perception of Canada as an independent operator, it would also affect our own perception of our independence. No overt American pressure would be needed to undermine this independence. Considering the economic costs that could be at stake, Canadians might well lose their will to follow their own inclinations in matters of foreign policy when they differed from those of the United States.

Perhaps Joe Clark had these and other considerations presented to him by his advisors at some stage during the government's examination of free trade, but if so the brief was very closely held. It is more likely that the economic dominance within the super-department would have been too strong and the predispositions of the government too well known for such an examination to have passed the ministerial triumvirate that headed External Affairs and to reach cabinet.

The movement of Canada into an orbit ever closer to the United States might be acceptable to many Canadians as a reasonable price for the material benefits expected from the Free Trade Agreement. After all, they might say, access to the US market will be worth much more to us than access to the Canadian market is to the Americans, and it is not unreasonable that we should pay something for the privilege. However, this was not a part of the public debate that preceded our implementation of the accord, and not only Canadians might be surprised by the changes implicit in Canada's position in the world.

As we move away from the precariously balanced policies required of a Middle Power to become a safely predictable ally, the old Canada will be missed by the international community. It might even be irreplaceable. Our ability to "do good" without being embarrassed about it, our detachment as a peacekeeper and our acceptability among Third World peoples will all diminish as our alignment with the United States becomes more obvious. It is a particularly great pity that this is happening at a time when bridgemakers, compromisers and a loyal opposition within our alliances are going to be needed to help shape a genuinely new world order. Indeed, if this depressing scenario were the only one imaginable, it would be a terrible tragedy. Fortunately there are others, if we can find a government with the courage to act on them.

Some Canadian government, some day, will have to face the diplomatic as well as the economic, cultural and social consequences of an agreement that means so much to one partner and so much less to the other. The separation of economic considerations from all other aspects of the Canada–US relationship is artificial: it will either break down on its own or be broken down. The agreement itself, however, probably cannot be undone or substantially renegotiated without incurring further losses. Canada's diplomatic independence will therefore best be served by finding a way of diluting American dominance of Canadian commerce before it becomes entrenched.

Fortunately there are signs that more broadly based trading arrangements may be emerging.

11

Other Options

When Brian Mulroney decided to leave office, like Pierre Trudeau before him, his parting thoughts were about foreign affairs. Trudeau's initiative has already been discussed; Mulroney's was quite different. For the latter, in addition to any other possible motives, there seemed to be a desire finally to cut an independent figure on the world scene. His friends, Messrs Reagan and Bush, had left the White House and been replaced by an unknown quantity. This might be a good time to add a little balance to his otherwise one-sided record.

In any event, Mulroney said some things about American policies regarding the former Yugoslavia that were less than totally supportive. In the circumstances, Mulroney's comments could have done damage (and probably not much good either), but they might have been meant to help his party in an election where its identification with the American agenda was potentially an issue. Like Trudeau before him, Mulroney's farewell performance might have been improved by a little professional advice. It would have been a great opportunity for advancing some considered suggestions on the future of the UN's involvement with peacekeeping and peacemaking.

The departure of Brian Mulroney will, of course, lead to a re-examination the Canada–US relationship, and probably in a way it had never been examined before. *Foreign Policy for Canadians* and the Third Option paper, produced for Trudeau, were less the result of an objective examination of the roots of foreign policy than they were attempts to find policies the new government could accept. No really substantial changes in policy emerged. The post-Mulroney review will have to start with the continentalist and trade-driven policies of that government and make an attempt to see where they have led, not just in economic terms but in terms of Canada's position in the world and *vis à vis* the United States.

In the Trudeau review, the policy that Mulroney later adopted of seeking closer contact with the United States was dismissed as a non-starter. In the coming new review, the existing policy will have to be the first option to be examined. For the first time the Free Trade Agreement might be looked at in its full political context. The new review will also look again at the North American Free Trade Agreement to include Mexico and, theoretically, other countries of the hemisphere.

It could well be found that an expanded free trade area would take some of the curse off the existing bilateral arrangement in that it would provide Canada (and any other members) with allies in their dealings with the United States. The fate of the proposed new arrangement, however, will not depend on the outcome of a foreign policy review but on the ability of its supporters to overcome the economic, environmental, cultural and social objections that have been raised against it in both Canada and the United States.

A second option to be considered in a new review would be to renounce the existing agreements, FTA and NAFTA both. Although there are those who advocate this on economic grounds, there are good political reasons for not doing so. First, there are no grounds for thinking that a unilateral cancellation of the existing agreements would take us back to pre-1990 days. Jobs that have gone south are not likely to return, but beyond that, it would be seen by some in the United States as an act of betrayal, undermining important long-term plans for the future of the hemisphere. Moreover, there are reasons for believing that the free trade deals may be superseded and their deleterious effects offset by changes in the works for the General Agreement on Tariffs and Trade (GATT). Indeed, under the Uruguayan Round of GATT, the opportunity to extend our trade, particularly in Asia, could reduce our existing dependence on the US market in spite of the FTA.

The new Third Option for Canada that might well emerge from a policy review would be to go flat out for a new GATT agreement (the Uruguay Round) and, concurrently, to extend our trading relationships with Japan, China and other growing marketplaces. Bearing in mind the experience of the previous Third Option, the new version would require a conscious and continuing effort to overcome the reluctance of many Canadian businesses to venture outside the North American continent, in spite of the fact that in some of these markets Canadians have some advantages over our American competitors in particular. In any fresh statement of government policy the government should assume responsibility for identifying and expanding markets in difficult areas, and not leave this up to individual businesses. When we bought into the American business philosophy we also left it to our business people to compete with American enterprise under their rules. Canadian entrepreneurs need (and used to get) strong support from government trade representatives abroad to offset the many advantages American traders have built into their own system: advantages that come from a business culture, control over multinational corporations (e.g. in trading with Cuba) and the diplomatic support of the world's only superpower.

To the extent that our commercial policy has been leading our foreign policy, it has already led us away from our role as a Middle Power on the world scene and toward, at best, a passive acceptance of American leadership. Not only did this save the government the trouble of making up its own mind on complex issues, it also obviated the possibility of a conflict with a powerful and hard-bargaining trading partner on whom we were increasing our dependence. The globalization of trade (as distinct from the continentalization of it) would broaden our trading options and enhance our bargaining position with all of our partners, including the Americans. It would not alter the fact that our ability to do business abroad depends on the productivity and imagination of our entrepreneurs and workers.

Although trade will continue to be a dominating consideration even after it has ceased to be the dominant one, and although economics may well go on shaping our relationship with the United States, business is not the only thing that matters. Even a foreign policy based on trade should take other factors of domestic and international life into consideration. In the modern world most of these factors are represented by international organizations — some regional, some worldwide, some concerned with very specific interests, some with broad political and strategic matters.

It has been an abiding element in Canada's foreign policy to join as many international organizations as it could and still play an effective part in each. The Organization of American States (OAS), a wide-ranging regional organization, was an exception until recently. Previous Canadian governments shied away from it at least partly because there was the risk that too much activity in an area the United States regarded as its backyard might have involved us in conflicts with the Americans on matters of no direct Canadian interest. Until 1989, Canadian governments had always decided that they did not need another area of potential conflict with the United States and confined themselves to observer status with the OAS. In that year, however, the government decided the risks were small and should be taken. Membership in the OAS does not seem to have led to any greater Canadian activity in the area. If, however, the larger hemispheric free trade area were to become a reality and we were to be a part of it, there would have to be a profound change in our attitude toward Latin America.

Canadian involvement in both la Francophonie and the Commonwealth have cooled under the Mulroney dispensation. Both organizations were considered by previous Canadian governments not only valuable in terms of domestic politics but also useful in our operations as a Middle Power; as sources of support in broader issues and conceivably helpful to us in maintaining the balanced relationship with the United States that was once a government objective.

Since the end of the Cold War, the *raison d'être* of Nato has been called into question. As an alliance created in response to Soviet expansionism, it was argued that it should have disappeared when the USSR did. Without subscribing to the contrary view, that the world is still a dangerous place and Nato should be preserved just in case, there is something to be said for maintaining the best international military organization in existence at a modified level of preparedness. Moreover if Nato is going to continue there are strong reasons why Canada should be a member of it. Events in the former Yugoslavia and the upheavals still going on in the former USSR should convince most people that military force is still a factor in world affairs. There is a question, however, concerning the circumstances in which Nato forces should be called upon to act. Although the alliance's members would naturally retain a veto over the use of their own forces, it would be consistent with Canada's past positions if a new government acted on the assumption that Nato would only consider military action if it were called upon by the United Nations.

The UN was, of course, where Canada established its position as a Middle Power, and it would be reasonable to expect that a future government would see that once again it became a focus for Canadian foreign policy. Through the decades of the Cold War, the UN was in eclipse and became much more a forum where the battles of the Cold War were fought than an instrument of international will. As a result many of its members, including the Great Powers, have written it off as a weak reed, a talk-shop rather than a place where things were done. During its eclipse, the UN's administration deteriorated and its Charter went unamended, further reducing confidence in the organization and making it more difficult for it to assume its proper place in international life. Both administrative reform and the revision of the Charter will have to be addressed.

During the dark days of the Cold War, Canada, through peacekeeping and by playing its full part in most UN operations, did much to preserve the UN idea for the time when it would be possible for it to function as at least some of its founders intended. It has therefore been particularly disappointing to see that, with the Cold War over, instead of trying to build the organization up so it might be given a significant part in the heralded new world order, the Mulroney government co-operated with the Great Powers in using the UN in much the same way as they had used it during the Cold War.

At the time of the Iraqi invasion of Kuwait the Security Council passed pre-negotiated resolutions but was not allowed to play even the largely titular role it had played at the outbreak of the Korean War in 1950. At that time the USSR had opposed any UN involvement, but it committed the blunder of walking out of the Security Council instead of staying and using its veto. This allowed the action in Korea to be taken in the name of the UN. Forty years later, for the invasion of Kuwait, the Russians were on-side and the Chinese turned a blind eye, but the UN was still permitted not even a titular role. It was asked only to rubber-stamp decisions that had been made elsewhere.

In the Korean case, the United States, very reasonably, would not place its troops under the command of the Security Council's Military Staff Committee, which included a Soviet member. Nevertheless, the Americans did allow it to be called a United Nations "police action." In spite of the greatly improved world climate, the Korean precedent was ignored by Ottawa in the summer of 1990 when Canada said "Ready, aye, ready," not to the UN, but to the President of the United States. Canadian ships sailed out of Halifax harbour to operate in the Persian Gulf, not as UN police wearing UN insignia under a UN flag, but as vigilantes; a posse of friends of the US who took it upon themselves to enforce a Security Council decision which they had sponsored but which had not yet been passed. It is doubtful if a Canadian government with such a profound stake in the US relationship would have thought it worth while to try acting on the Korean precedent, or even wait for UN approval, given the importance the Gulf Expedition played in the thinking of the Bush administration.

Here was a case of the Canadian initiative *manqué,* a precedent that bodes no good for the future for the international community's part in the operation of a new world order. A new Canadian government would want to review Canada's commitment to the United Nations to see if a different precedent could be created that would at least see that the United Nations was somewhere near the centre of peacekeeping and peacemaking operations being carried out on behalf of the international community.

The United States is not the villain in an otherwise wonderful post–Cold War world. For their own valid national reasons, none of the historical Great Powers have shown the slightest enthusiasm for enhancing the part to be played by the UN in the new world situation. In the events following the breakdown of the former Yugoslavia, the UN's role was confined to that of mobilizer of peacekeepers. The role of peacemaker has moved around but remains open. In future, a Canadian government might want to make sure its forces were not be committed to dangerous "peacekeeping" operations until they were accompanied by interconnected arrangements for peacemaking and a committment by the international community that it intended to see both activities through to an agreed end — the equivalent of what would be called "war aims" in a different context.

Although the Great Powers alone have the essential resources for dealing with situations like that in the Balkans, they do not normally have a sufficient identity of interests to be able to agree on any single course of action. In Kuwait the interest — oil — was there. Only when perceived interests have been called into question (the Falkland Islands or Panama, for instance) are the Great Powers likely to use their military resources outside their own borders.

The countries that usually have the greatest interests in containing conflicts like the one in the Balkans are the smaller neighbours, other countries that can imagine comparable problems arising in their own areas and still others that have vested or other interests in a peaceful world. These countries, not the Great Powers, are most likely to want to see measures taken to restore international peace and security. Given some leadership, they are the countries that could shame or otherwise force the hands of the Great Powers through initiatives in the UN.

In the Balkans, for instance, it would have taken no great exercise of ingenuity to have devised a programme based on the existing Charter of the United Nations to isolate the belligerents, find means of helping refugees, deny the victor any spoils based purely on recent conquest and, when the war was over, arrange for the investigation of those who had defied the United Nations or committed other recognized crimes. The problem has not been a lack of ingenuity, only the habit of waiting for leadership from those whose other interests prevent them from leading. No great mobilization of public opinion would be needed nor would there have to be an international conference on the subject. All that is needed is action in the UN by a group of like-minded middle and smaller powers on an agreed set of measures that applied the principles of the Charter to the Balkan situation and which the Great Powers could be cajoled or shamed into supporting.

Although the nature of the international political system that will replace the Cold War is still undetermined, it is not too early to say that it must be based on more than a collection of regional powers combining for limited purposes to deal with issues as they arise. The planet's environmental problems cannot be dealt with other than globally and neither can its political problems, as we have seen in Kuwait, Somalia and Yugoslavia, and may yet see in the former USSR. Moreover, the revival of market economies strongly suggests that there really is such a thing as a world economy in which different economic areas will have to find their appropriate places.

Canada will have little choice but to play a modest part in all of these areas — political, military and economic. Whatever happens to the present attempt to create an American regional trading group, Canadians should continue to see themselves as world, not regional, traders. Middle Power status was tailored to suit Canada's geopolitical and economic situation as well as its collective personality and it has called for a degree of cussedness in not accepting solutions or even "facts" as they are presented to us by the Powers, even by our friends.

There could be no greater diplomatic challenge for Canadians than to see that our foreign operations are treated as a whole under a single national diplomacy; to see that future decisions will be made on the broadest view of the public interest. If a future government decides to follow this course, it will need to rearrange the way in which foreign affairs are managed. It will require an agency very much like the Department that once was.

The new super-department, which changed its name in 1989 to External Affairs and International Trade, Canada, is itself something of a scrambled egg, and trying to unscramble it in a rush might do more harm than good. For the short term, at least, to implement a more broadly based foreign policy it would be sufficient for the new government to reassert the right of the Secretary of State for External Affairs, not a triumvirate, to be consulted on any matter of international interest that he or she considered likely to affect more than one Canadian interest on the international scene. Moreover, the minister and people directly responsible to him or her should become the centre of responsibility for the day-to-day management of Canadian operations abroad to ensure consistency and co-ordination among them.

It is devoutly to be hoped that a future prime minister will be less concerned about putting a personal imprint on the foreign policy of Canada than he or she will be in pursuing the foreign policy objectives that have served this country so well since its emergence on the world scene in the 1940s. Our prosperity has gone hand in hand with our willingness and ability to play an independent and responsible role as a member of the world community. So have our self-respect and the respect of the international community. Some of us have been seduced by visions of grandeur or wealth into thinking we could compete with the United States on its own turf and in its own entrepreneurial specialty. In pursuing their illusion, they allowed the country to be led away from its traditional paths, diminishing Canada's international stature and leaving its cultural roots exposed to the elements.

It is particularly sad that all this uprooting was undertaken by people who called themselves Conservatives and claimed to be the heirs of John A. Macdonald and Robert Borden, both of whom chose the harder path along which Canada had found a destiny of its own. Nevertheless, the facts of geography and history as well as economics that dictate Canadian foreign policy remain, in spite of the great changes that have taken place in the world around us and, indeed, in our own way of looking at them. A new government will be taking a fresh look at these same facts and attitudes. There is every reason to assume that it will come up with a different set of answers.

12

... And a New Earth

A fresh survey of Canada's interests in the world at the end of the twentieth century would identify two main themes: one of a country of the Western Hemisphere, neighbour and ally of the dominant power of our times, and the other of a Middle Power on the world scene. Canada's welfare, and perhaps the welfare of some other countries, will depend on how a future government brings these two themes together in an integrated foreign policy whose components do not conflict but support each other. The concept of foreign policy as the extension of domestic policy into the international environment, could be invoked to help determine the relative position of the two themes.

The dominant domestic imperative of Canadian life is the preservation of the country's national unity, challenged as it is by the demands of a bilingual and multicultural society. One of the elements of that society, without which the country probably could not exist, is the province of Quebec, whose primary political role is to preserve its French culture. One of the problems Quebecers have with Canada is that they see very little difference between their anglophone compatriots and their anglophone southern neighbours. They might also note a diminishing desire on the part of the other Canadians to preserve the differences that do exist. Those Quebecers who think in this way might well conclude that Quebec is already alone on a great anglophone sea and that such shelter as they used to get against the full force of American culture is diminishing under growing pressures from the south.

Many English-speaking Canadians, if not a majority, do not accept this Quebec assessment about the inevitability of the anglophones' assimilation into a North American melting pot. These people would be willing to pay a considerable price to maintain the existing differences between Canadian and American society. The survival of Canada as a distinct society on the North American continent is thus linked to the survival of French Canada as a distinct society. Both

require future Canadian governments to see that the forces of assimilation are contained. This central domestic fact should be given its
full weight when foreign policies come up for consideration. What
we do abroad must not only be consistent with our domestic needs,
but our actions must also be complementary and mutually supporting
in the way they protect and advance the country's domestic and
external interests.

Some thoughts on the future economic relationship with the
United States were offered earlier. But there is also a need for
Canadians to deal with at least one philosophical aspect of the American connection. Canada has been mercifully free of dogmatism in its
politics. Even those Canadians who call themselves socialists have
behaved pragmatically, no doubt because of the need to get elected
and, when in office, the need to hold on. With the defeat of Soviet
communism, there has been a tendency to assume that if that ideology was a lie then its chief opponent, free enterprise capitalism, must
be the truth. The most ardent supporters of the free market as an
economic system have recognized that a free-market mechanism if
left alone would soon destroy itself; hence anti-combine legislation
and the criminalization of insider trading. The free market is indisputably the best economic system available for our purposes, but in
Canada it has never attained the standing of a sacred principle.

In Canada most reasonable people will allow that the economy is
a means to an end, not an end in itself, and that private entrepreneurs
should not always be the first recipients of their own products,
including profits. Swedish social democracy for many, many years
gave the country's businesses the freest possible hand in producing
goods and making profits, which were then taxed to maintain the
welfare state. In the United States, however, "free enterprise" is more
than just an economic system, it has been identified with democracy
itself. This ideological attitude has been moving north. It threatens
the hitherto successful mix of private enterprise with public responsibility to produce, among other things, the Canadian social safety
net, health care and a degree of burden sharing.

It is important that in our relations with our neighbours we do not
subscribe to their purer economic philosophy, not just on principle,
nor to preserve a difference but because our system was evolved to
meet our special circumstances which differ from theirs and which
would not be as well served by American models. In our dealing with
the United States at the end of the twentieth century we should keep
reminding ourselves that even that great country is only a part of the

world scene. Environmental and other issues of truly global propor-
tions are closing in on all of us. Canadians will have to decide
whether they want to respond globally or in accordance with regional
interests.

A new world was given to us in 1989, a veritable *annus mirabilis,*
when one of those great unpredicted events brought forty years of
Cold War to an all-but-instant stop. In spite of many running sores,
the world was released from the long-standing threat of Mutually
Assured Destruction and was allowed to dream of things like "peace
dividends." Now for the first time ever, it is possible to imagine a
really new world order that could address, not just the continuing
international conflicts, but the other traditional enemies — pesti-
lence, hunger and inhumanity.

In spite of many, many words to the contrary, instead of a new
world order, the old order has been reaffirmed, based on the use of
military power in the hands of sovereign states. War or the threat of
war was broadly acceptable while there was still a superpower run
by people who professed to believe that violence was a necessary
virtue through which their version of Utopia would be created. But
with that system gone bankrupt, the place of military power either to
maintain a form of peace or for the settlement of disputes needs to
be redefined.

It would be hard to overstate the importance of the United Nations
in Canadian foreign policy or, to be honest, the important part Canada has played in the preservation and enhancement of the UN itself.
It would be folly to throw all of that away and allow Canada to
become a part of a more restricted vision of a world of regions with
the old rules still applying.

That meaner vision is a real possibility. The one-battle war that
might better be known as the Persian Gulf Punitive Expedition made
it clear that even a veto-free United Nations would not be trusted to
do what it was created to do for the preservation of world peace and
security. What was to pass for the enforcement of international law
and order would be selectively determined by what served the foreign
(and indeed the domestic) policy interests of the only surviving
superpower. Even worse, there was no international player on the
scene ready to point out the obvious: that the UN should be more
than a rubber stamp. It was a role that a different Canada might have
screwed up its courage and played.

In truth, the winding down of the Cold War has presented anew
some of the problems that were merely deferred when World War II

was followed, not by a peace, but by the Cold War. The frontiers outlined at Yalta have come unstuck and the large military components in our economies, for the first time since 1939, are worried about their survival. As co-operation replaced confrontation some fundamental institutions have had their futures questioned. Battering ram at the ready, the nations of Nato stand before an open door and wonder what to do with it. It is hard to shift gears downward. How much of the energy we were willing to put into our own defence do we want to put into the defence of others? Can peace and security be maintained without the overt use of force? Is anyone ready to find out if religious, racial and ideological hostilities would really fade away if they were not nourished by injustice? Or because there was no possibility of impartial adjudication? If all the answers are negative then international security will continue to depend on the selective and self-interested policies of the great military powers and history will be on the way to repeating itself.

Probably the greatest challenge for the industrialized countries lies within the former Soviet empire. The origins of the Cold War are gone but the suspicions it produced are still in place. In spite of enlightened American policies, it would be unreasonable to expect that the United States in particular would act to restore the successor of the USSR as once again a military or economic rival. Yet as the components of the old Soviet empire stew in their own vitriol more running sores are being created and on a scale that could make the world forget all the others.

One thing emerging is hopeful. If the Confederation of Independent States or its major components are to survive they will probably be vaguely democratic and, where appropriate, federalist. Since democracies rarely wage war on each other, the existing democracies should find a way to help East European governments democratize themselves. That means helping them look after the minimal needs of their populations.

It so happens that Canada first staked its claim to sit at the same table with the Great Powers in a situation that was very similar to the present one. At the end of World War II, Canadians insisted that their participation in policy decisions about relief and rehabilitation in Europe had to be accepted along with their wheat. In any future world order there will be a need for a few "floaters" — well-informed diplomatic operators who do not subscribe to any particular view of political or economic orthodoxy but who are willing to pay their dues and able to encourage the voices of reason, particularly those that may be having difficulty in being heard in their own countries.

These were things Canada did very effectively in co-operation with like-minded countries — the Scandinavians, Australia, New Zealand and others. No Great Power is going to encourage any country to play the gadfly, but the role is a necessary one and it can be played with an effect out of all proportion to the importance of the country doing it, provided it is not seen as a cat's-paw for one of the principal players. It was in this area that the Department developed special skills and had an acknowledged reputation. Presumptuous as it may be to say so, without a Canada that is seen to be its own personality, there is a danger that there will be no gadflies willing to work for a really new world order. The Gulf expedition showed what happens when the Great Powers are left unharried to arrange things in their own short-term interests.

There are alternatives. If there is to be a world order rather than a *pax imperialis* then it should be managed at least in the name of the UN, especially when military force is contemplated. It should be the UN's responsibility to define both political and military objectives and to see that they do not neutralize each other, as they did in Iraq where, after the smoke cleared away, the offending government was still in power.

The coming struggle in the UN may well be about the extent to which it may take action which in another era would have been regarded as an impermissible intervention in the domestic affairs of a member state. In Iraq, in Somalia and in the former Yugoslavia, action taken in the name of the UN did involve such domestic intervention. It will be important that such action is limited to instances where the Charter of the UN has been violated and that any action taken should be seen, not as the action of a self-interested third party, but as an act on behalf of the overwhelming majority of the members of the international community. UN action could be anything from an offer of its good offices, through the "excommunication" or "banning" of offending governments (as distinct from states), to a declaration of non-belligerent war (militarily enforced blockade and diplomatic isolation) between the offending regime and the UN acting as the sole agent of the international community. Even if for practical reasons any necessary military action had to be assigned to member states, it should be done in a manner that made the United Nations' participation unmistakably clear, beginning with the display of its symbols and insignia.

In the context of the situation in the former Yugoslavia, the UN was given the thankless job of being peacekeepers where none of the belligerents wanted peace kept. The stronger belligerent parties wanted to keep the fighting going because they thought they would win, the weaker because they had no reason to believe the would-be peacekeepers could or would protect them. Peace*making* was a totally separate matter.

While all this was going on, nothing came out of New York because those who were providing troops, including Canada, never asked for or suggested clear terms of reference in terms of militarily attainable objectives that would probably have had more to do with saving lives than settling frontiers.

In a world just freed from the nuclear nightmare, the litany of human anguish goes on. In purely humanitarian terms, Africa's needs are greater than any others, and they deserve attention on that basis. But Africa does not have the destructive power at its disposal that Eastern Europe still has and, cruel and unfair as it is, it will not get the detailed and continuing political attention that will be given to Eastern Europe and the Middle East. All developed countries will argue the same way; they must first ensure their own security before they can help others, and they will do that come what may. Since their own security is more closely linked militarily and economically to what is going on in Europe and the Middle East than it is with Africa, that will be the order of their political priorities. Humanitarian aid for Africa will, sadly, continue to concentrate on tiding over the crises rather than on dealing the underlying problems. No doubt any Canadian government would continue to be involved on the same basis.

Since the Golden Age of External Affairs, a number of new items have come on the international agenda. With decolonization came international development, to be followed by environmental issues and, more recently, human rights. In all of these, Canada's concern is a mix of direct self-interest and the sort of do-goodery in which it has long specialized. Concern for human rights, once a forbidden area because it suggested interference in the internal affairs of another country, has become a part of the process of economic development. And development by its very nature is closely linked to environmental problems. As matters stand, it would be bold enough to suggest that a foreign policy for the coming century would require that these interrelationships were internationally acknowledged.

Looking back over the years during which the Department reached the peak of its influence, it seems as if Canada had a destiny to be in all things a Middle Power, an agent of influence for moderation in the geopolitical middle; a crossroads and entrepôt, politically, ideologically, culturally, commercially and spiritually. Over the same period in its own political life, the country was a laboratory, testing ways in which regional, cultural, social and economic diversity could be maintained and still permit political co-operation; its unity is a unity based on differences, not merely tolerant of them. In a world that must learn very quickly how to protect the interests of the planet and still respect different national ones, Canada should create its own agenda based on its middleness. Learning from its own diplomatic history, Canadians should set about doing the things they can do on their own, internally and externally, and not rely on their ability to persuade. Paradoxically, that has been the way they have been most successful in influencing others.

It is a cliché but there's no harm in repeating it: If the multinational state cannot be made to work in a country as well placed as Canada, it cannot be made to work anywhere. If thinking people in any of the many political circles that make up this country have decided that Canada is a purely economic phenomenon, a cross between a milch cow and a collective bargaining unit but not really a state, then its future is already decided and the details can be left in the hands of its receiver.

On the other hand, if Canadians want their country to survive as a member of the international community, the choice will be between acting as a part of a team led by a Superpower or in following its own destiny as a Middle Power. If the decision is to opt for the comfortable obscurity of team membership, there is no need to change direction; that is where the country is headed. However, if we prefer the Middle Power option, a new government might do worse than remember that once upon a time there was something called the Department of External Affairs.

Index

Achevé d'imprimer
en novembre 1993 sur les presses
des Ateliers Graphiques Marc Veilleux Inc.
Cap-Saint-Ignace (Québec).